Turkish Migration Conference 2015 Book of Abstracts

I0093463

Transnational Press London
2015

Turkish Migration Conference 2015 Book of Abstracts

First Printing: 2015

Paperback

ISBN: 978-1-910781-15-9

London, United Kingdom
www.tplondon.com
www.turkishmigration.com

Contents

SESSIONS

**Turkish Migration Conference
Programme & Abstract Book**
25th – 27th June
Charles University Prague, Czech Republic

Welcome to TMC 2015

The Turkish Migration Conference 2015 is the third
event in the series, we are proud to organise and host
at Charles University Prague. Perhaps given the growing number of participants and variety in scope of
research and debates included at the Conference, it is
now an established quality venue fostering scholarship
in Turkish Migration Studies.

Turkey has recently and suddenly turned into a major
destination country with the arrival of over 2 million
Syrians and Iraqis fleeing the crisis in the region. There
has been already strong flows of Turkish origin migrants and returnees from Europe as well as flows of
transit and asylum movers. Turkey and its international partners therefore faces new challenges in managing
migration to, from and through Turkey.

Over the last four years, we have seen over 600 abstracts submitted to the conference and year on year
the number of accepted presentations grew by about
15 percent. This year, we will be together with about
200 academics from all around the World and enjoy
about 150 presentations, each refereed by two review-
ers. The Turkish Migration Conference attracting such
a healthy number of academics is a good indicator of
the success and means the conference serving its pur-

pose and offer a good opportunity for scholarly exchange and networking.

I would like to thank all our colleagues who serves on the conference committee, hundreds of authors who also reviewed substantial number of abstracts and papers so far. We thank to Charles University Prague for hosting the event. We also thank to our supporters University of California Davis Gifford Centre for Population Studies, Manisa Celal Bayar University Faculty of Economics and Administrative Sciences and Center for Population and Migration Studies, Regent's University London Centre for Transnational Studies, Univerziti Publishing, Transnational Press London, for their support and contribution to the Conference.

Prof Dr Ibrahim Sirkeci
Conference Chair and Ria Financial Professor
Director of Regent's Centre for Transnational Studies
Regent's University London, United Kingdom

E-mail:
sirkeci@yahoo.com & sirkecii@regents.ac.uk

Aims and Scope of TMC 2015

The TMC 2015 is devoted to investigating Turkish migrant dynamics and patterns, migrant experiences, the costs of migration, as well as the economic, social, educational and cultural outcomes.

Including contributions from scholars and students from anthropology, demography, business, economics, psychology, sociology, political science, geography, development studies, law and other disciplines, the conference provides a forum through which to consider all aspect's related to Turkish migration around the world.

Contributions from comparative perspectives have been particularly welcome too. Adopting an interdisciplinary approach to migration dynamics and patterns, and by drawing on comparative studies of international and internal migration process, the TMC 2015 includes contributions covering country of origin, transit and destination countries focusing on human mobility from, to and in Turkey as well as studies on other migration cases from around the world.

Caroline B. Brettell

Professor Caroline Brettell is Ruth Collins Altshuler Professor and Director of the Interdisciplinary Institute at Southern Methodist University, Dallas, USA. She holds a Ph.D. from Brown University. Caroline Brettell joined the faculty of Southern Methodist University in 1988. In 2003, she was named Dedman Family Distinguished Professor and in 2009 University Distinguished Professor. She served as Director of Women's Studies from 1989-1994 and as Chair of Anthropology from 1994-2004, as well as Dean ad Interim of Dedman College, 2006-2008. She is currently serving as the Ruth Collins Altshuler Director of the Interdisciplinary Institute in Dedman College. She received her B.A. in Latin American Studies from Yale University and her M.A. and Ph.D. from Brown University. In 2000-2001, she served as President of the Social Science History Association and between 1996 and 1998, she was President of the Society for the Anthropology of Europe (SAE). She served as President of the SMU Faculty Senate and at the SMU Board of Trustees in 2001-2002. She has also served as a member of SNEM-3 Scientific Review Panel, National Institute of Health (1999-2003). Among her research interests are: migration and immigration, the cross-cultural study of gender, the intersections of anthropology and history, and European ethnography, particularly Portugal. Other interests include ethnicity, historical demography and family history, kinship, and the anthropological study of religion.

Jeffrey H. Cohen

Professor Jeffrey Cohen's research focuses on three areas: migration, development and nutrition. Since the early 1990s he as studied the impact, structure and outcome of migration from indigenous communities in Oaxaca, Mexico to the US with support from the National Science Foundation. He has also conducted comparative research on Mexican, Dominican and Turkish migration. His work on traditional foods, nutrition and migration was supported by the National Geographic Society. In addition to ongoing work in Oaxaca, he is currently studying the migration of Mexicans to Columbus.

Nedim Gürsel

Gürsel is an award winning Turkish author. He is a graduate of the Sorbonne's Department of Modern French Literature. His has completed his PhD dissertation on Louis Aragon and Nazim Hikmet. In 1977, Gürsel's A Summer without End won the Prize of the Turkish Language Academy. In 2008, Gürsel published The Daughters of Allah. Gürsel is a founding member of the International Parliament of Writers. He teaches contemporary Turkish literature at the Sorbonne, and works as the research director on Turkish Literature at the International French Science Research Center (CNRS). Gürsel's awards also include the Abdi Ipekçi Prix (1986), the Freedom Award by French PEN Club (1986), Haldun Taner Citation (with Tomris Uyar and Murathan Munhan) (1987), Struga Gold Plaque Award (1992), France-Turquie Literary Prize "Fernand Rouillon" (2004), and Art and Literature Chivalry by French Government (2004).

Douglas S. Massey

Professor Douglas Massey is a professor of Sociology at the Woodrow Wilson School of Public and International Affairs at Princeton University. His research focuses on the sociology of immigration with particular emphasis to North America. He received his B.A. in Sociology, Psychology, and Spanish, from Western Washington University in 1974, and in 1977 he received an M.A. in Sociology from Princeton University. Massey holds a PhD from Princeton University. Douglas S. Massey is the founder and co-director of the Mexican Migration Project and the Latin American Migration Project, with his long-time collaborator Jorge Durand. Massey was president of the Population Association of America in 1996. He served as the 92nd president of the American Sociological Association, 2000–2001.

Since 2006 he has been president of the American Academy of Political and Social Science.

Philip L. Martin

Philip Martin is Professor of Agricultural and Resource Economics, Chair UC Comparative Immigration & Integration Program. Philip Martin received his degree from the University of Wisconsin-Madison in 1975. His research focuses on: immigration, farm labor, and economic development. Martin is Chair of the University of California's Comparative Immigration and Integration Program, and editor of the monthly Migration News and the quarterly Rural Migration News. Martin has earned a reputation as an effective analyst who can develop practical solutions to complex and controversial migration and labor issues. In the U.S., he was the only academic appointed to the Commission on Agricultural Workers to assess the effects of the Immigration Reform and Control Act of 1986. He received UC Davis' Distinguished Public Service award in 1994. Heassessed the prospects for Turkish migration to European Union between 1987 and 1990, evaluated the effects of immigration on Malaysia's economy and its labor markets in 1994-95, and Martin was a member of the Binational Study of Migration between 1995 and 1997. In 2001-02, he assessed the options for dealing with unauthorized migration into Thailand.

The Venue:
Charles University Prague Jinonice Campus

Charles University's Jinonice campus is only a few paces from Jinonice Metro Station which is served by Yellow Line and about 5-6 stops from the city centre. To help plan your stay in Prague, tourism guide for Prague can be found here: www.praguewelcome.cz/en/

Charles University Jinonice Campus

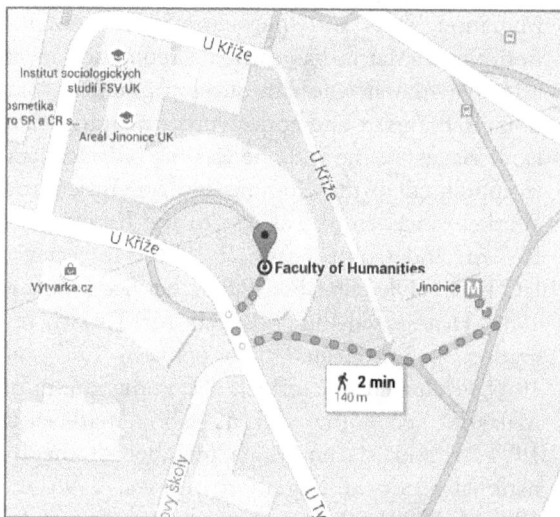

Conference Committee

- ❖ Prof Ibrahim Sirkeci (Chair), Regent's Centre for Transnational Studies, Regent's University London, UK
- ❖ Prof Philip L. Martin (Co-Chair), Dept. of Agricultural & Resource Economics, University of California, Davis, USA
- ❖ Dr Wadim Strielkowski (Co-Chair), Faculty of Social Sciences(Co-chair), Charles University Prague, Czech Republic
- ❖ Dr Inna Čábelková (Co-Chair), Faculty of Humanities, Charles University Prague, Czech Republic
- ❖ Prof Ali T. Akarca, Department of Economics, University of Illinois, Chicago, USA
- ❖ Dr Bahar Baser, University of Coventry, UK
- ❖ Prof Gudrun Biffl, Department of Migration and Globalization, Danube University Krems, Austria
- ❖ Dr Elias Boukrami, Regent's Centre for Transnational Studies, Regent's University London
- ❖ Prof Jeffrey H. Cohen, Department of Anthropology, Ohio State University, USA
- ❖ Prof Dilek Cindoğlu, Department of Sociology, Artuklu University, Turkey
- ❖ Prof Ali Caglar, Department of Political Science, Hacettepe University, Turkey
- ❖ Dr Mehmet Ali Dikerdem, Institute for Work Based Learning, Middlesex University, UK
- ❖ Dr M. Murat Erdoğan, Migration and Politics Research Centre, Hacettepe University, Turkey
- ❖ Dr Tahire Erman, Department of Political Science, Bilkent University, Turkey

- ❖ Prof Sibel Kalaycıoğlu, Department of Sociology, Middle East Technical University, Turkey
- ❖ Dr Altay Manco, l'Institut de Recherche, Formation et Action sur les Migrations, Belgium
- ❖ Luisa Morettin, Regent's Centre for Transnational Studies, Regent's University London
- ❖ Dr Assia S. Rolls, Faculty of Business and Management, Regent's University London
- ❖ Dr B. Dilara Seker, Department of Psychology, Celal Bayar University, Turkey
- ❖ Dr Levent Soysal, Faculty of Communications, Kadir Has University, Turkey
- ❖ Prof Aysit Tansel, Department of Economics, Middle East Technical University, Turkey
- ❖ Dr Ali Tilbe, Namik Kemal University, Turkey and Regent's University London, UK
- ❖ Dr Östen Wahlbeck, School of Social Science, University of Helsinki, Finland
- ❖ Dr Pinar Yazgan-Hepgul, Department of Sociology, Sakarya University, Turkey
- ❖ Dr M. Murat Yüceşahin, Department of Geography, Ankara University, Turkey
- ❖ Dr Welat Zeydanlıoğlu, Kurdish Studies Network, Sweden
- ❖ Dr Sinan Zeyneloğlu, Department of City and Regional Planning, University of Gaziantep, Turkey

Local Organisation Committee
- ❖ Dr Wadim Strielkowski (Co-Chair), Faculty of Social Sciences, Charles University Prague
- ❖ Dr Inna Čábelková (Co-Chair), Faculty of Humanities, Charles University Prague

- ❖ Dr Tuncay Bilecen, Regent's Centre for Transnational Studies, Regent's University London
- ❖ Dr M. Rauf Kesici, Regent's Centre for Transnational Studies, Regent's University London
- ❖ Burcu Oskay, Regent's Centre for Transnational Studies, Regent's University London
- ❖ Prof Ibrahim Sirkeci, Conference Chair & Director of RCTS, Regent's University London
- ❖ Dr Güven Şeker, Population and Migration Research Centre (NUGAM), Celal Bayar University, Turkey
- ❖ Therese Svensson, Regent's Centre for Transnational Studies, Regent's University London
- ❖ Fethiye Tilbe, Regent's Centre for Transnational Studies, Regent's University London

Supporting Organisations

- ❖ Charles University Prague, Faculty of Humanities
- ❖ University of California Davis Gifford Center for Population Studies
- ❖ Regent's University Centre for Transnational Studies
- ❖ Manisa Celal Bayar University, Population and Migration Research Centre
- ❖ Manisa Celal Bayar University, Faculty of Economics and Administrative Sciences
- ❖ Migration Letters journal
- ❖ Göç Dergisi journal
- ❖ Kurdish Studies journal
- ❖ International Economics Letters
- ❖ University Servis Publishing
- ❖ Transnational Press London

Conference Structure

The TMC 2015 is held over three days, with each day comprising of 4 parallel sessions of oral presentations. Registration will open at 08:30 on Thursday the 25th June 2015. Parallel sessions will run from 09:00 or 09:30 each day.

There will be three plenary sessions; one in each day of the Conference. In plenary sessions we will hear talks from Douglas Massey, Caroline Brettell, Philip L. Martin, Jeffrey Cohen, Nedim Gürsel and other distinguished panellists.

The Conference Dinner will be held on the Saturday from 19:00 at Plzenska Restaurant, located in beautiful premises of the old Municipal House downtown Prague. During the dinner the Best Paper Prizes will be presented.

TMC 2015 Schedule

	Thu 25th Jun	Fri 26th Jun	Sat 27th Jun
08:30	Registration opens		
09.00		Parallel	
09.30		Sessions 4	Parallel
09:45	Welcoming		Sessions 7
10:00	speeches		
10:30	&	**Break**	
10:50	Plenary	Parallel Ses-	
11:00	Session A	sions 5	**Break**
11:20			Parallel
12:00	**Lunch**		Sessions 8
12:20		**Lunch**	
12:50			**Lunch**
13:20	Parallel		
14:00	Sessions 1	Plenary	
14:10		Session B	Plenary
15:20	**Break**		Session C/
15:40	Parallel		PSD
16:00	Sessions 2	**Break**	
16:10			**Break**
16:20		Parallel	
16:30		Sessions 6	Parallel
17:10	**Break**		Sessions 9
17:30	Parallel		
18:00	Sessions 3		
18:20			
19:00			Conference
21:00			Dinner

Programme Summary

THURSDAY 25th June

Parallel Sessions 1. 13:20 - 15:20

A. Integration Processes
B. Business, Economics and Immigrants
C. Göç ve Edebiyat
D. Syrian Movers in Turkey

Parallel Sessions 2. 15:40 - 17:10

A. Europe in Turkish Migration Policy
B. Irregular Migration and Remittance
C. Göç ve Sürgün Edebiyatı
D. Migrant Identity

Parallel Sessions 3. 17:30 - 19:00

A. Integration, Harmonization, Marginaliza-
    tion
B. Family Formation and Migration
C. Göç ve Uyum
D. Migration Policy and Perceptions
E. Internal Migration

FRIDAY 26th June

Parallel Sessions 4. 09:00 - 10:30

A. Return Movements

B.   Circassian Diaspora
C.   Kamu Yönetimi Açısından Göç
D.   Gender and Sexuality

Parallel Sessions 5. 10:50 - 12:20

A.   Counter-Hegemonic Migrant Spaces,
      Place-Making and Resistance
B.   Demographic Analysis of Migration
C.   Yeni Göç Eğilimleri
D.   Migration in Literature

Parallel Sessions 6. 16:20 - 18:20

A.   Migration and Religious Identity
B.   Kamu Hizmetleri ve Göç
C.   Türkiye'de Göç ve İşgücü Piyasaları
D.   Integration and Identity

SATURDAY 27th June

Parallel Sessions 7. 09:30 - 11:00

A.   Between Naturalization and Irregularity:
      Migrants and (Il)legal Membership in
      Turkey
B.   Politics and Migration
C.   Integration and Identity
D.   Spatial Productions of the Social: Identi-
      ty, Subjectivity and Power

Parallel Sessions 8. 11:20- 12:50

A.   Integration in Europe
B.   Migrants of Istanbul

C.   Migration and Literature
D.   Identity in Kurdish Migration

Parallel Sessions 9. 16:30 - 18:00

A.   Public Opinion and Syrian Movers
B.   Edebiyatta Göç ve Kimlik
C.   Education and Migration
D.   Conflict and Politics in Kurdish Migration

Conference Dinner & Best Paper Prizes

19:00 – 21:00 Plzenska Restaurant
               Closing notes by Prof Jeffery H. Cohen
               Presentation of Best Paper Prizes

Sharing Bread in the Local Brussels Vicinity

(43) Johanna M.L. Kint (University of Technology Eindhoven)

With this paper we present an ongoing, participative and social design project taking place in the Brabantwijk of Brussels. At its final stage, the Sharing bread project will have four outcomes: Breadbox, Gained Bread, Bread Oven and Bread Exchange Station. This paper covers the starting up of the project with the 'Urban Rituals' workshop and co-creation sessions with the local community of the Brabantwijk.

The sharing bread ritual was investigated by closely observing informal urban activities that are performed on a daily basis in several streets of the Brabantwijk. Turkish merchants from this neighbourhood share their old bread with other inhabitants. This ritual finds its origin within the Islamic culture, where old bread may not be thrown away. Bread is treated with reverence throughout the Muslim world. Mistreatment of bread is a sign of disrespect towards the source of all sustenance. This tradition of not throwing bread away has a great, not yet developed potential in this Brussels area, as the bread initially is set apart from the garbage in the street, but finally ends up as mere waste.

By developing these four project outcomes we aim to give this meaningful bread ritual a new visibility and sustainable place within social urban life. What are these four projects about? Breadbox refers to the design of a box where the local community can automatically deposit its bread in a hygienic way. Gained Bread is about the development of an installation, converting deposited and unused bread into bio-energy. Active participation and social dialogue in this multicultural neighbourhood is stimulated by means of a public Bread Oven. Bread Exchange Station works as output station archiving, exhibiting and organizing a wide range of lectures and workshops, to informing people more technically on the fermentation process for gaining energy.

***

Turks in German Political Life: Effects of Turkish Origin Politicians to Integration

(3TP) Tolga Sakman (Turkish Asian Center for Strategic Studies (TASAM))

Turks living in Germany for over fifty years now the elements of their countries have become permanent. Assets in Europe as a result of the persistence of Turkish society and made many attempts to demand certain rights, political participation as it carried out the most logical way.

Prerequisites for participation in political life in Germany were examined and this study was started with the framework of competencies which Turks have and may have in this condition. In order to examine the political activity of the Turks comes to political participation should be to look at the organization of the basic movements. Individual participation in social and political preferences, and this choice affects a lot remains to be general criteria. In addition this article contains that how religion, identity, prejudice and homeland – host country dilemma constitute an obstacle to political participation of the Turks. This study includes some public opinion researches and surveys, action and discourses of Turkish politicians in Germany and some studies from literature of migration studies. Thus, a historical perspective was used while investigating of the present and future of Turkish participation to German political life.
***

Psychological Processes of Acculturation of Turkish/Muslims in Germany

(157) Hacı-Halil Uslucan (University of Duisburg-Essen)

In the last years, there is a very stable assumption in the public discourse in Germany that the process of social integration of Turks as an ethnic group and Moslems as a religious group has failed. Problems with head scarf, honour murderings, juvenile violence acts, higher unemployment rates or lack of german language competencies are even shown as valide indicators for this assumption.

This article will at first sketch the psychological process of acculturation, focusing on the topic of managing cultural and religious diversity on the individual level. Then, in the next step, the question of measuring and quantifying of acculturation processes will be examined for having an empirical access to this kind of overstreched socio-political claims.

At least, we will present some of our own empirical results about Muslim pupil and their acculturative strategies/orientations in Germany. The article ends with some suggestions how to overcome hindrances for a better social integration of this group.
***

Facets of African immigrants' mobility in Greece: Between transnationalism and integration

(116) Apostolos G. Papadopoulos (Harokopio University of Athens) and Laukia-Maria Fratsea (Harokopio University of Athens)

Despite that in the last two decades Greece was rapidly transformed to a destination country for immigrants, the unprecedented crisis has had a severe impact on immigrants' settlement and integration. New migrant flows which originate from Asia and Africa have induced new challenges for the national authorities and policy makers in Greece. Usually oriented to the countries of Western Europe, migrants from Africa and Asia, pass through Turkey and cross the Greek border in a search for better living opportunities in Europe. Turkey plays an important role as an immigration hub for a number of reasons. In the midst of the economic crisis many of these migrants have never managed to find employment in the country and their greatest care has been to move to the rest of Europe.

The paper presents the findings of a recent empirical research conducted in the period 2011-2013 which aimed at the investigation of the migration process as well as the prospects of African immigrants' integration in Greek host society. In total 532 questionnaires addressed to immigrants originating from seven sub-Saharan African countries were collected, while 53 interviews were conducted with second generation African immigrants, state agencies, migration policy institutions and civil society organizations. The main aim of the paper is to map out the migration process of African immigrants as well as to investigate the various dimensions of their social and geographical trajectories in the country. Starting from seven different Sub-Saharan

African countries, we examine the 'journey' of African migrants through Turkey to Greece, their expectations, the routes they followed and their integration prospects into Greek society. The distinction between different 'types' of African mobility shed light to the migratory strategies of African immigrants, which interact with structural and institutional factors.

***

Embodiment of Recognizing Differences: Alevis in Germany

(106) Deniz Coşan-Eke (Munich Ludwig-Maximillians University)

Alevism is mostly defined as a heterodox and syncretic belief system associated with Anatolian folk culture. Along with the Alevi community at both the national and the transnational level, Alevism have recently been influenced and transformed by an increase of transnational migration. It is in this transnational and national space that the current article seeks to explore the current struggle for recognition through Alevi organizations and the meanings of recognition of Alevi identity in Germany, by analysing the teaching of Alevism and Equal Rights Agreements in some Federal States of Germany. Information has been gathered using participant observation of Alevi Associations in Munich, Hamburg and Stuttgart from 2011 to 2013. The research aims to provide opportunities for identities to be renewed by recognition of differences, and why the recognition of their differences is important for Alevis.

***

SESSION 1B – Business, Economics and Immigrants

Migration – Trade Nexus Revisited: Evidence from Turkish Migrants in OECD Countries

(144) Kadir Karagöz (Celal Bayar University)

In recent decades, economists seek to find the answers of two very fundamental questions "why has world trade grown, and what are the consequences of that growth?". Two sources that come to mind immediately are trade liberalisation and falling transportation costs. Another possible explanation is that trade has grown because economies have converged in economic size. A fourth source may be increased outsourcing. And as another factor the international movement of people may play a significant role on international trade. The declining cost of travel and communications has lowered information barriers and encouraged migration across national borders.

The current paper aims at testing the impact of migration on bilateral trade in an augmented panel gravity model framework. To this end the relationship between Turkish emigrant stock in the 13 OECD countries and bilateral trade volume (imports and exports) for the years 2000 – 2012 was analysed. Economic size and geographical distance between trading partners were controlled. Preliminary results show that there is a significant impact of migration on bilateral trade both in terms of imports and exports. On the other hand, as expected, economic size and distance have positive and negative effect respectively on trade.

***

Production of Turkishness in Relation to Small Food Businesses in Germany

(70) Anlam Filiz (Emory University)

In 2009, Thilo Sarrazin, a member of the Social Democratic Party of Germany (SPD), and former member of the Executive Board of the German Central Bank, declared that migrants had failed to integrate. Arab and Turkish migrants, he argued, had no productive value except for their vegetable trade, referring to the various grocery stores owned and managed by migrants. In 2011, murders of 10 migrants in Germany between 2000 and 2006 were revealed to be conducted by NSU (Nationalsozialistischer Untergrund). The media named the murders as "döner murders." Both of these events were named discriminatory and received backlashes from migrant communi-

ties and anti-racist groups. This article analyzes how Turkishness is constructed in relation to small food businesses in the cultural imaginary of Germany. It does so by analyzing the reception of the two major events mentioned above, which connected Turkishness with the food industry, i.e. Sarrazin's interview about integration and the naming of NSU murders as "döner murders" by the media. The article analyzes the representations of the Sarrazin debate between 2009 and 2011 and NSU murders between 2011 and 2013 in five major newspapers in Germany, the liberal-conservative Frankfurter Allgemeine Zeitung, the centrist most widely circulated weekly Die Zeit, the best-selling daily tabloid Bild, center-left wing Süddeutsche Zeitung and cooperative-owned left-wing daily die Tageszeitung. The article provides insights about the construction of migrant identities and ethnicities by majority populations.
***

Analyzing the Shopping Expenses of Turks While Abroad within the Context of Credit Card Usage

(6TP) Yağmur Özyer (Arel University), Alper Değerli (Beykent University), Başak Değerli (Marmara University) and Ebru Gözükara (Arel University)

It is possible to say that reflections of some terms like glocalization and transnationality of which recognitions are growing across the entire world within the last quarter of the 20th century are increasingly experienced in in today's our interactive world. While technologic improvements and social transformations are narrowing the boundaries countries, the scope of transportability is widening to a great extent. This period of change have also caused the differentiation of the shopping perceptions and shopping from abroad have turned gradually from luxury expenditures that only <u>high income group</u> can afford into standard necessities. Besides these developments, presence of credit cards which eliminate the obligation of holding cash facilitate shopping practices free from the exchange problem in a different country. In this study, credit card usage of Turkish consumers of which usage penetration is growing inceasingly was analyzed and tried to comment investigating whether this usage level takes place in a specific pattern statistically.

***

Measuring Attitudes towards Augmented Reality Practices on Transnational Consumers

(5TP) Alper Değerli (Beykent University), Başak Değerli (Marmara University), Nevin Karabıyık (Marmara University), Aytaç Uğur Yerden (Gedik University)

Especially in recent years, progressive improvements in technology have seperated augmented reality from a science-fiction element and these kind of practices have started to take part increasingly in our daily lives. Although teleportation technology is still an utopia, with a simulative copy of real it becomes possible to feel "as if being there" through augmented reality experiment. McLuhan's statement "*technology is an extension of the human body*" may even shape beyond his notion, our eyes experience a place for miles away as if being there. Thus, it's estimated that expreriencing the place planned to visit in detail and gaining detailed information will grow the necessary information before the experiment and this experiment in question will be conducted more effectively. On the other hand, it can be seen that augmented reality practices also effect mobility and transnational consumption. Accordingly, transnational consumers' prefer to have an experience about a different country before visiting it or not is significant for both transnational marketing and augmented reality technology. In the scope of this study, it's aimed to research if potential transnational consumers who live in Turkey intend to use augmented reality practices before going somewhere and their attitude towards these practices. Within this context, gained results have been presented and, tendency and attitudes of transnational consumers to the augmented reality practices have been tried to specified.

***

Analysing Turkish Labour Migration to Europe via SWOT and STEPLEE

(125) Hasan Akça (Çankırı Karatekin University)

In order to send Turkish labour to foreign countries, Turkey signed migration agreements with Germany in 1961, Austria, Netherlands and Belgium in 1964, France in 1967, and Australia in 1968. Main purpose of these agreements was to find job for unemployed Turkish people and contribute to economies of European countries. Over the 50 year period of time, the situation has changed. Today, some Turkish people have contributed to Germany as entrepreneur, traders, representatives of NGOS, officers instead of labour.

The aim of this study is to explain reasons for Turkish labour migration to European countries, determine likely effects of Turkish migrants on economies of both Turkey and Germany, to present expectations and difficulties of migration via SWOT and STEEPLE. These analyse techniques take a photo of Turkish labour migration to Europe point of view of Socio-cultural, Technological, Economic, Ecological, Political, Legal and Ethical.

***

Menekşe Toprak'ın Öykülerinde Almanya'ya Göç'ün Farklı Yüzleri

(59) Nesime Ceyhan Akça (Çankırı Karatekin University)

Göçmen bir ailenin iki kültürlü çocuğu olarak büyüyen Menekşe Toprak, ilk ve ortaöğrenimini Köln ve Ankara'da yapar. Ankara Üniversitesi Siyasal Bilgiler Fakültesini bitirdikten sonra Ankara ve Berlin'de dört yıl kadar bir bankanın elemanı olarak çalışır. 2002 yılından günümüze gazetecilik ve çevirmenlik yapan yazar, Berlin ve İstanbul'da yaşamaktadır. Hikâyeleri Almanca, Fransızca, İtalyanca ve İngilizceye çevrilen genç yazar, bu ülkelerin edebiyat dergilerinde ve öykü antolojilerinde yer aldı. Hâlihazırda iki öykü kitabı (Valizdeki Mektup,YKY 2007; Hangi Dildedir Aşk, YKY 2009) ve iki romanı (Temmuz Çocukları, YKY 2011; Ağıtın Sonu, İletişim 2014) vardır. Yazarın tüm eserlerine sinen ana izlek "bir yere ait olma hissi" olarak belirlenebilir. Yoksulluğun çözümü olarak görülen ve yaşanan göç, yeni mekâna ulaşıldığında ve yaşama koşullarına asgarî oranda adapte olunduğunda esas problemler gün ışığına çıkar. "Türklerin büyük Almanya göç"ünün bir parçası sayabileceğimiz Menekşe Toprak'ın yaşadığı ve şahit olduğu hayat parçalarından sızan öyküler, geride kalanları, yıllar sonra bir arada yaşamaya yeniden alışmak zorunda kalan parçalanmış aileleri, zamanla değersizleşen işçi emeğini, göçmen işçilerin ortaya çıkan yahut gizlenen direnişlerini, ikinci kuşağın kendini gerçekleştirme arzusunu, iki kültüre sıkışan aşkı ve hepsinden fazla iki ülke arasında bir yere ait olamama hissini yakalamaya çalışır. Biz bu bildirimizde Menekşe Toprak'ın öykü kitaplarında (Valizdeki Mektup, Hangi Dildedir Aşk) karşımıza çıkan göç sorununu, disiplinler arası bir bakışla edebiyat sosyolojisi penceresinden irdelemeye çalışacağız.

***

Cumhuriyet Dönemi Romanlarında Ekonomik Nedenlere Bağlı İç Göçe Dair Bir Tahlil Denemesi

(62) Polat Sel (Trakya University)

İç göçler zihinde ilk uyanan anlamıyla bir ülkenin sınırları içerisinde köy, kasaba veya şehirden bir başka köy, kasaba ya da şehre doğru yapılan göçlerdir. Göç etme eylemi kırsal kesimde yer alan yerleşim birimlerinden daha büyük yerleşim birimlerine doğru olabileceği gibi büyük yerleşim birimlerinden daha küçük yerleşim birimlerine doğru da olabilmektedir. İç göç, geçmişten günümüze kadar olan süreçte tarih, ekonomi, sosyoloji, antropoloji, psikoloji, siyaset bilimi gibi birçok farklı disiplin tarafından çeşitli yönleriyle ele alınmış ve ele alınmaya devam eden bir kavramdır.

İç göç hadisesine sebep olan pek çok etmen vardır. Bunların en önemlileri arasında ekonomik, toplumsal, siyasi, kültürel sebepler ile savaşlar gelmektedir. Bu konu yukarıda saydığımız beşerî ve toplumsal bilimler dışında edebiyat sahasında da kendisini göstermiştir. Biz bu çalışmamızda iç göç olayının meydana gelmesinde etkili olan temel belirleyici etmenlerden ekonomik sebeplerin kurgusal bir metin olan roman düzlemindeki yansımalarını metinler bağlamında ortaya koymaya çalışacağız.

***

Orta Asya'dan Balkanlara Son Türk Göçünü Gerçekleştiren Peçenek, Uz ve Kumanların Göç Yolları ve Kültürel Etkileri

(68) Fatma Rodoplu (Trakya University)

Tarih boyunca insanlar başta ekonomik nedenler olmak üzere siyasi, sosyal ve dini sebeplerle bir coğrafyadan başka bir coğrafyaya göç etmişlerdir. Çok uzun bir tarihi geçmişe sahip olan Türkler de ilk ortaya çıktıkları Türkistan sahasından Sibirya, Anadolu ve Orta Avrupa'ya kadar göç faaliyetleri içerisinde yer almıştır. Türklerin göç hareketi genellikle batı istikametinde olmuştur. Kitleler halinde gerçekleştirilen Türk göç hareketlerinin başlıca sebepleri kuraklık ve hayvanlar için yeterli otlak alanların bulunamamasıdır.

Peçeneklerin Batı Göktürk Devleti'nin VII. yüzyılda dağılmasından sonra Karlukların güçlenmesi neticesinde Talas boyundan Sır Derya'nın aşağı tarafına doğru gittikleri görülmektedir. Ural ve Emba nehirleri boyunda yaşayarak Hazarlara komşu olmuşlardır.

Peçenek, Uz ve Kumanlar Orta Avrupa'nın içlerinde sonlanan uzun göçleri sırasında başka etnik unsurlarla karşılaşmışlar ve birçok devletle siyasi mücadelelere girmişlerdir. Bu Türk kavimlerinin Karadeniz'in kuzeyine gelişleri Rusya, Doğu ve Orta Avrupa tarihinde önemli bir değişime sebep olmuştur. Bilhassa Balkanların etnik açıdan gelişmesine ve çeşitlenmesine yol açmıştır. Bu çalışmamızda söz konusu kavimlerin izledikleri göç yolları ve bu yollar üzerinde bıraktıkları kültürel izler ele alınacaktır.

***

Yahya Kemal'de yolculuk ve şiirin varoluş serüveni

(137) Pınar Aka

Yahya Kemal 1903-1912 yılları arasında dokuz sene boyunca ülkesinden uzakta, Paris'te yaşamıştır. O yıllarda Türk entelektüellerinin gitmeye can attığı bir kenttir Paris. Yahya Kemal için de bu yolculuk, her şeyden önce kültürel bir zorunluluktur. Ancak o, Fransız kültüründen ve genel anlamda Batı medeniyetinden etkilenmekle birlikte, kendi kültürel mirasını gözardı etmeyecek

ve Paris'te Osmanlı şiirini ve tarihini inceleyecek, kültürel kimlik meseleleri üzerinde derinden düşünecektir. Diğer taraftan, Yahya Kemal'in yolculuğunun kişisel ve psikolojik bir boyutu da vardır. Bu boyutun en önemli bileşenini şairin henüz on üç yaşındayken kaybettiği annesi oluşturur. Bu yazıda, Yahya Kemal'in yolculuğunun nasıl şiirsel bir yolculuğa dönüştüğü, metaforlar üzerinden gösterilmeye çalışılacaktır.
***

Göç Yollarinda Ulaşim Araçlari (1968 öncesinde)

(33) Yılmaz Buktel (Trakya University)

1968 yılı, bu bildiri için iki farklı önemli noktaya işaret eder. İlki Mercedes – Benz lisansıyla Türkiye'de ilk defa fabrikasyon olarak şehirlerarası ve şehiriçi otobüs imalatının başladığını gösteren bir kuruluşun faaliyete geçmesidir. İkincisi ise Yaşar Kemal'in eserinden uyarlanan 1968 yılı yapımı Urfa – İstanbul filmidir. Bu filmde günün şartlarında ve günün ulaşım araçlarıyla yaşanan bir kaçma-kovalama öyküsü perdeye aktarılmıştır. Konumuz itibarı ile bizi filmde kullanılan ulaşım araçları ilgilendirir. Bildiri genelinde ise amaçlanan, 1950 yılında tek parti iktidarının değişimiyle başta "Taşı Toprağı Altın Şehir" İstanbul olmak üzere Anadolu'nun büyük illerine doğru yoğunlaşmaya başlayan göç yolları ve göç araçları üzerinde durarak 50'li ve 60'lı yıllarda Türkiye'nin ulaşım koşullarını (hava - deniz ve kara yolları) irdelemektir.

***

SESSION 1.D. – Syrian Movers in Turkey

Refugees of a City: The Socio-Spatial Impacts of Those Syrian Refugees Who Arrived in Izmir (Turkey)

(8) Arife Karadağ (Ege University)

The mass demonstrations which originated in Tunisia and then spread to Egypt, Libya, and the other Arab countries and defined as 'the Arab Spring' soon led to changes in regime in these countries, and they have also spread to Syria since March 2011. The rebellions in Syria and the reflections of the Arab Spring in Syria gradually turned into a human crisis upon the severe interventions of the Assad regime in the opponents and civilians. Doubtlessly, both Syria and the countries neighboring Syria were substantially affected by these conflicts and exposed to a serious flow of refugees in the same process. Likewise, it is expressed that the number of Syrian refugees who have arrived in Turkey since April 2011 has exceeded 1 million (USAK, 2013).

The first group of Syrian refugees that arrived in Turkey (252 people) entered through the Hatay border on April 29, 2011. When 2013 arrived, however, this figure reached 1 million, with 200,034 of them living in 21 refugee camps on our borders and about 750,000 of them living primarily in our border cities and nationwide. Although there is no organized camp in İzmir, our study area in the paper, it is known that the total number of refugees who particularly live around the bus station of the city and in neighborhoods such as Mersinli, Çamdibi, Pınarbaşı, Altındağ, Doğanlar, and Naldöken or in neighborhoods affiliated to Konak and Çiğli has exceeded 200,000, with 90 000 of them being registered (The Governorship of İzmir, 2013). Mardin constitutes one pillar, and the case study of İzmir constitutes the other pillar, of the two-stage project study on "Refugees of a City: Socio-Spatial Impacts of Syrian Refugees on the City", directed at our department by me. The results of the fieldwork carried out in the Kızıltepe, Mardin pillar in February 2014 will be shared in the 2014 Annual Congress of the National Association of Geographers (June 2014, Muğla). On the other hand, it is intended to present the results of the part which constitutes the second pillar of the project and which we jointly perform with the Provincial Directorate of the Migration Administration of the Governorship of İzmir and the Department of Foreigners in the Police Headquarters in İzmir during the 5th Symposium on Urban and Regional Research Network.

The spatial changes that have occurred at the metropolitan center of İzmir, where the Syrian refugees who were headed for Turkey following the events experienced first during the Arab Spring and then in Syria settled down temporarily but for an uncertain period, will be addressed in the paper that is planned to be presented in the congress. Later on, the socio-economic impacts on the everyday life of the city and particularly the quality of urban life, urban services, job & employment and security problems will be discussed comparatively from the perspectives of the Syrian refugees and the local people of İzmir. The statistics and reports obtained from the Turkish National Police and the AFAD (the Disaster & Emergency Management Presidency) constitute the main sources of these evaluations. In addition, the results of the comparative analysis of the data collected via the questionnaires applied to some 200 Syrian refugee families and the same number of İzmirian families that were reached with the fieldwork carried out in the districts where the Syrian refugees were concentrated at the metropolitan center of İzmir will be shared with the participants of the symposium. Finally, it will be intended to express the expectations of the Syrian refugees who are going on their lives at the metropolitan center of İzmir and of the people of İzmir, the scene for socio-spatially significant changes upon the arrival of the Syrian refugees whose number has skyrocket-

ed for the last one year, in this process and the problems they are confronted with.
***

The Role of the Ngos in the Field of Refugee Protection in Turkey in the Light of Ongoing Relations with the State

(73) Pınar Cereb (Middle East Technical University)

The main objective of this paper is to understand the difficulties of the NGOs in Turkey in the field of refugee protection and their limits in terms of finding durable solutions to the refugee problems and to discuss the role of the state with respect to take inititative in this regard. Interest for conducting such a thesis, that takes the limits of NGOs as a problem to find durable solutions in the field of refugee protection has three main sources. First of all, during the last decades, it has been observed that the realm of refugee protection has been expanded in Turkey as the conflicts around the region increased especially after the war in Syria. Houndreds of thousands of people left their countries and came to Turkey to seek asylum and they face many challanges during their stay in Turkey. From health issues to sheltering, NGOs were given crucial role to provide basic needs of refugees and to protect their rights. With the increase number of asylum seek-

21

ers, NGOs came to a point that it is no longer enough to leave refugee protection in the hands of NGOs. During the implementation, NGOs faced many problems which they cannot handle with these problems by themselves. Although NGOs continue to make improvement, in order to find more durable solutions, the more active role of the state is needed.

In this sense, the relation between NGOs and the state which started to be seen as symbiotic should be researched. In order to understand the role of NGOs in general and their aims and objectives in the field of refugee protection in terms of their capacities, related literature should be looked into. The legal documents and their implementing institutions in Turkey will also be examined in order to understand the relations between the state and the NGOs in terms of refugee protection. In addition to that, to understand their roles in the field of refugee protection in Turkey and their difficulties to meet the needs, seven NGOs in the field will be interviewed.
***

Perceptions about Refugees in Turkey: An Evaluation on Newspaper Coverage of Syrian Refugees

(92) Filiz Göktuna Yaylacı (Anadolu University) and Mine Karakuş (Anadolu University)

Academic studies have increasingly been focusing on the phenomena of migration and emigration as well as developments related to them. Turkey became an emigrant country with the emigration process that started in the 1960s. Over the course of last fifty years, many academic researches have been conducted about people who emigrated from Turkey particularly to Europe. Lots of stories covering those emigrants have been appeared in newspapers in different contexts. Among the majöre themes of these stories are the success or failure of emigrants, and their problems concenring integration, discrimination, xenephobia, racism and prejudice. In recent years, as a result of certain social, political and economical developments, Turkey has gradually become a transition country for the undocumented migrants. At the same time Turkey now is a reciever country in the context of international migration. Especially due to the conflicts in Syria and Iraq, Turkey became one of the most important destination countries for the mass refugee flows. Social, political and economical reasons prompt and create different reactions and perceptions about Syrian refugees. In this context, the way newspapers or other media outlets cover developments concerning Syrian refugees gains notable importance. Newspapers shape social perceptions in certain ways while reflecting the public perceptions about refugees. To examine and analyze these news could help us

understand the perception about migration and migrants and refugees from a different angle particularly in the case of Turkey. Along the lines outlined above, this study seeks to understand the perceptions about Syrian refugees as reflected in the coverage of newspapers in Turkey. To this end, the study was designed as a qualitative research, and document analysis method was used for data collection. As part of the study, news stories covering Syrian refugees from Hürriyet, Milliyet, Sabah, Sözcü, Birgün and Yeni Şafak dailies between 1 January 2014 and 31 December 2014 were analyzed on the basis of themes, styles, main concepts, photographs, and etc. Six newspapers are selected as samples according to their political standing as pro-government, oppositionary and impartiql main-stream. Among oppositionary newspaper, Cumhuriyet are analyzed; among pro- government, Yenişafak, and among mainstream, Hürriyet dailies are analyzed.
***

Effects Oo Problems of Pre-Migration and Post-Migration Processes on Syrian Women Refuges' Mental Health

(147) Veli Duyan (Ankara University), Elif Gökçearslan Çifçi (Ankara University), Fulya Akgül Gök (Ankara University) and Ezgi Arslan (Ankara University)

During the recent years there has been a turmoil in Middle East, especially in Syria and this turmoil causes forced migration. Migration affects human life deeply from very different ways. Migration is a complex process affected individuals' life socially, economically and physically. Generally people migrates because of education, accessing better job opportunities, family problems or wars. Syrian refugees who temporally lives in Turkey, have experienced socio-cultural, physiological, educational, vocational and health problems because they take refuge in Turkey.

Hardships of migrations can create serious and devastating results in terms of emotional functionality (Akinsulure-Smith ve O'Hara, 2012). Migration processes may result in physical and mental health problems (Gaber ve diğ., 2012). According to Akinsulure-Smith and O'Hara, migrants suffers mostly from medical, occupational, linguistic, legal problems and luck of social work services (2012). Difficulties in adaptation to migrated place, social and legal systems of new placement, language and cultural differences can cause some mental health problems. Some research shows that migrated populations have more psychosocial and health problems than local populations (Virupaksha et all., 2014).

It is generally believed that migrants are more vulnerable to mental problems because of the experience of migration itself, cultural adaptation, and a disadvantage socioeconomic position (Knipscheer ve diğ., 2006). Women are one of the groups who experienced pre-migration, during migration and post-migration problems mostly. They have traumatic experiences like violence, tough living conditions and domestic conflicts (Measham et al, 2014). Furthermore foreign language, cultural and social differences, social exclusion and labeling can cause psychological problems. Kirmayer et all have found that women migrants do not seek help for their mental health. They have stated that this can be the result of luck of information and reluctance to discuss problems outside the family (2011). In the World the number of female migrants is increasing in recent years (World Migration Report, 2010). It can be said that women affect more severely. Psychosocial well-being of an individual consists of social, physical and psychological components. Apart from physical health, mental health issues are also serious problems for migrants. It's known that most of the Syrian refugees experienced torture, rape, kidnap, murder and massacres; because of that these people's mental health have been affected severely (James et all., 2014). Mental health services for women should be a priority. So the mental health problems of Syrian refugees should be determined for creating above mentioned mental health services.

This study is aimed to determine the experiences from during migration and post-migration processes and the effects of these experiences on psychology of Syrian women refuges who temporally lives in Turkey. This study is planned as a qualitative research. Syrian refugees will be contacted from Social Solidarity and Support Associations in Ankara, Turkey.

***

Future Expectations of Young Syrian Immigrants and Their Social Support Perceptions

(149) Elif Gökçearslan Çiftçi (Ankara University), Münevver Göker (Ankara University) and Tuba Yüceer Kardeş (Ankara University)

Trying to find a living space for themselves in Turkey due to migration, the Syrian immigrants face a number of psycho-social, economic, political and cultural problems. The Syrian refugees that have problems with meeting their basic needs primarily such as sheltering, health and education after the migration are unable to use the employment opportunities and social resources equally with country's citizens due to the language barrier, cultural differences and social prejudices; and they may experience intensive stress, anxiety and depression. The period before, during and after the migration is undoubtedly experienced by children and the young at maximum. In the process of migration, children and the young have traumatic experiences due to war like the loss of family and relatives, separation from caregivers, exposure to violence, challenging life conditions, insufficient nutrition, contagious diseases and domestic conflicts (Measham et al, 2014). Migration may be more challenging for the young who are in a period of challenging developmental duties, compared to adults. Young immigrants face a number of barriers like acceptance in the foreign country, racism, inclusion in a peer group and language problem (Cooke, 2008; Tanyas, 2012).

Future perceptions of the young who are forced to leave their country due to forced migration are shaped by these negative conditions. Various studies show that the positive future perception is especially associated with advanced social and emotional development among minority and low-income young (Werner&Smith, 1982). In this context, it is suggested to analyze the future perceptions of child/young immigrants according to their states of using educational, sheltering, health and employment opportunities, as well as their family conditions, residence permit, access to services and exposure to discrimination in the process of adaptation to the Turkish society.

The process of migration causes the change and weakening of domestic dynamics and social relations in various contexts. Migration is known to bring along disruptions, restrictions or qualitative changes in social support networks (Hovey, 2000; Aronowitz, 1984). Social relations and social approval that shape the social support perceptions of adolescents have a very important place in their lives; however, migration causes them to be destitute of this support (Gün and Bayraktar, 2008). Thus, both the forced migration and the process of adaptation to the foreign country and the culture considerably affect the future perceptions and social support perceptions of young immigrants. Children/young are in a need for social support especially in the process of coping with intensive changes and adapting to the new culture.

This study aims to determine the future expectations and social support levels of young Syrian immigrants aged 15-35, who have come to Turkey due to the forced migration and migrated to the city of Ankara instead of living at a camp, and are under temporary protection. The study has planned to access to the contact information of Syrian immigrants via the Social Assistance and Solidarity Foundations. Quantitative method will be used in the study. The Turkish questionnaire form will be translated into Arabic and be applied to young Syrian immigrants in intensive regions.
***

The Transformation and Europeanization of Migration Policy in Turkey: Multiculturalism, Republicanism and Alignment

(129) Bianca Kaiser (Kemerburgaz University)
and Ayhan Kaya (Istanbul Bilgi University)

This paper will scrutinize the historical forms of managing migration and diversity in Turkey, as well as the development of the Europeanization process of Turkey's migration policy. The paper will be arguing that managing diversity in Turkey can be historicized in three epochs: Ottoman multiculturalism, Turkish republicanism, and the contemporary model of Europeanization. Turkey has so far witnessed both multiculturalist and republicanist forms of integration being implemented respectively by the Ottoman state and the modern Turkish state. The Millet system of the Ottoman Empire meant that the state was officially recognizing the existence of religious communities and granting them group rights. Whereas the modern Turkish state became republicanist through its difference-blind constitution, underlining individual rights, and denouncing group rights. However, the Kemalist state has never been truly a republicanist state, as it partly continued the Ottoman Millet system favouring the Sunni-Muslim majority at the expense of other identities. In this paper, the author will concentrate on the ways in which the Ottoman state and the modern Turkish state have tried to manage diversity in Anatolia. The main premise of the paper is that the Ottoman form of managing diversity was based on the rhetoric of tolerance, which is actually loaded with a lot of problems subjecting the other to the benevolence of the majority society – a rhetoric which was first put into action by the Ottoman Empire in the Balkans in the 15th Century. Republican Turkey, on the other hand, is based on the equality of all citizens irrespective of ethnicity, religion, gender, and age, with an aim of homogenizing the nation in a way that resulted in the fact that the act of migration and the diverse nature of the society at stake have been almost completely denied. This also includes the denial of the fact that contemporary Turkish society is mainly composed of migrant origin populations - a fact that has even been denied in national school curricula of national education since the early 1930s.

While most laws and regulations pertaining to Turkey's immigration regime were mainly made during the early years of the Republic, they have come increasingly under scrutiny. In an effort to keep up with the transformation of Turkey from a country of emigration to a country of immigration and, at the same time, to align Turkish laws with the EU's acquis communautaire, a reform

process has started in the late 1990's, and is still going on today. The dynamics underlining this process, ie. alignment with the EU's acquis communautaire, have culminated in a new and comprehensive law in April 2013. The Law on Foreigners and International Protection acknowledges the need to structure the emergence of an integration sector. The dynamics of the Europeanization process will be outlined by concentrating on legal immigration. It will be underlined that while Turkey has become one of the most interesting cases among countries which have recently transformed into important immigration destinations, the country is still at the beginning of a long policy-making road and public debate. The paper will conclude with the depiction of the new Law of Foreigners and International Protection as a legal document referring to the fact that Turkey has become a country of immigration, and will include with some policy recommendations.
***

EU-Turkey Readmission Agreement: Not A"Carrot" But More A "?"

(41) Ülkü Sezgi Sözen (University of Hamburg)

The regional instability, especially in Syria, Iraq, Afghanistan, Palestine, Pakistan and China, irregular migration to Turkey increased significantly. Many migrants try to continue their journey towards the EU, but many others, especially Syrian people stay in Turkey because of the new economic opportunities there. Therefore, the migration policy has recently become a priority issue not only for the EU but also for Turkey. It is essential to point out the importance of the cooperation with the neighboring countries. Only the prevention of the EU's borders cannot be successful until the neighboring countries cooperate in the fields of irregular migration and the fight against cross-border criminality and terrorism. In order to this, the EU should offer a certain level of inclusion in the form of economic privileges or visa facilitation. It was to this end that the EU signed a Readmission Agreement also with Turkey and initialed the Roadmap towards visa liberalisation as a compensatory measure. The aim of this paper is therefore to explain the Readmission Agreement between the EU and Turkey and discuss some potential impacts of this agreement not only from the EU's perspective but also from Turkey side. In order to this, after a short introduction, Turkey's EU journey will be explained. Secondly, the competence of the EU on signing an international agreement on behalf of its Member States will be clarified. Thirdly, the genesis and scope of the Readmission Agreement between the EU and Turkey will be handled. In addition to this, the Roadmap towards a visa-free regime will be emphasized. Finally, as conclusion, some potential

impacts of this agreement on migration policy will be interpreted and discussed.
***

A Multi-Level Analysis of the European Union Immigration and Asylum Policy Concerning Irregular Transit Migration and Its Implications for Turkey

(111) Ela Gokalp Aras (Gediz University)

In recent years, while the migratory movements have been imposing dramatic changes on the existing national and international policies in this field; irregular migration and in particular irregular transit migration from transit countries to the destination countries attracts ever-increasing and considerable attention since 1990s.

In order to control its external borders and to respond the shortcomings of the existing policies in the Member States, the European Union (EU) has been implementing different policies and policy instruments regarding irregular migration, where 'externalization' appears as the main characteristic as referring moving borders to third countries and establishing partnership with countries of origin and transit. In case of irregular migration, delocalization is used for the control of this type of migration and supported by securitization and economisation discourse. In this framework, the EU uses external dimension of its immigrant policy as a mode of governance and adopts different policy instruments and tailor-made measures for each country for operationalization. While the EU imposes different measures to each country; the consequences and the reaction are also diverse in the concerning countries. As a sending, receiving and most importantly transit country; Turkey supplies a significant settlement to analyse the implications of the externalities of the EU's policy in irregular migration.

This study analyses the implications of the EU's immigration and asylum policy concerning irregular migration in Turkey as adopting a multi-level and multi-sited approach. In this framework, this study focuses on the implications of the concerning policies on the normative and institutional changes as well as implementation dimension in Turkey at macro level; implications on irregular migration related social networks in the specific gateway cities (multi-sited ethnography in Edirne and İzmir) at meso level and finally, examines the policy implications on the migration experiences of the irregular transit migrants at micro level.

Within this study mainly the 'interpretative approach' is adopted and qualitative research methods, mainly the 'ethnography of policy analysis' is employed to understand how the relevant actors and institutions receive, interpret, implement and affected by the concerning policies.

During the data collection also secondary sources and the existing statistics were benefited; however the main method that lights the way for the findings of this research can be seen as the field research, which is conducted from August 2011 to March 2013 in Ankara, Edirne and İzmir, where at macro level 18, at meso level 78 and micro level 11 in total 107 semi-structured interviews as well as in-depth interviews and participant observations were realized with the policy implementers and policy receivers.
***

Europeanisation and Turkish Migration Policy Reform: From Accession to Policy Conditionality

(81) Birce Demiryontar (University of Sussex)

Until the adoption of the visa liberalisation road map in December 2013, The EU have been influencing migration policy reform in Turkey through accession conditionality. However, it is difficult to state a substantial progress as both parties have reduced their efforts towards accession to a bare minimum. The discontinuation in the country's accession process, caused a halt in the EU induced policy change in other policy areas in Turkey, and a similar halt was expected for migration policies as well. The EU have prevented this halt by presenting visa liberalisations as an incentive which is solely dependent on the

progress in the migration issue area. This paper aims to explain this transformation from the accession conditionality to policy conditionality and argues that this new policy conditionality framework specific to migration-related issues not only ensured the sustainability of the reform agenda but also accelerated it. In the EU accession negotiations in which the parties were stuck in a deadlock, the persistence on using the accession conditionality as a negotiation term have been counterproductive. Thus, here, the migration policy negotiations between Turkey and the EU are illustrated with an aim to demonstrate the possibility of a relation among the parties, outside of accession conditionality. These issue area specific relations, are indeed more efficient to reach a negotiated agreement, in comparison to accession conditionality. Thus, this kind of relationship is promising the shape the future of the EU-Turkey relations in other issue areas as well.
***

SESSION 2B – Irregular Migration and Remittances

Why Do the Norms Matter in Struggling With Irregular Migration at Sea? The Case of Boat People on the Aegean

(95) Özlen Çelebi (Hacettepe University)

Irregular migration is vitally important and mostly neglected aspect of international migration. Since last two decades the volume and the numbers of people involved in worlwide irregular migration movements have increased. In parallel, measures to prevent irregular migration by the destination countries have become more severe. Irregular migration is perceived as a security issue by most of the states and some international agencies. It can be claimed that irregular migration can hardly be a security problem for states. However, it is a security issue for most of the irregular migrants if we think that they are on the move because of economic, social or political insecurity experiences they have had in thier home or the previous host countries. Nevertheless, perceiving irregular migration as a security issue leads the erosion of the fundemantal rights of migrants. International migration policies of states can function as keys to analyse the dynamics of international politics. International policies to deal with irregular migration reveals how states in the 21st century got stuck with threats to national security which could be introduced by "foreigners." Irregular migrants, however, are usually not dangerous foreigners who could challenge the security policies of any state. They are themselves are in need of support and protection against dangers threatening their lives. They are vulnerable to fatal threats while passing throeug the land or sea borders of a country in an irregu-

lar way. This study claims that they are irrgular not illegal persons and they are prone to threats especially in a plastic boat at a sea. This study also aims to analyse the basic aspects of Turkey's struggle with irregular migration. As having in mind the fact that there are almost two millions of Syrian refugees in Turkey besides refugees from Iraq, Afghanistan and countries, and refugees from these countries compose the majority of irregular migrants who are vulnerable to deadly and dangerous situations at East Mediterranean, Turkey's combat with irregular migration and cooperation between international actors should be also a live-saving operation at the coast of the Aegean Sea. Numbers of irregular migrants on rise and insufficient level of international cooperation which has structured by misperceptions and judgements leave the refugees in a limbo where there is usually no respect to norms. This study aims to describe why do we need norms in migration management and why norms do matter.
***

The Social Life of Remittance Houses: Scenes from Rural Kayseri

(76) Oguz Alyanak (Washington University)

This paper examines the social life of remittance houses. It traces how building these houses are central to masculine narratives among migrant men, and explores the ways in which the changing function of these houses can be perceived as a challenge to these narratives. Based on ethnographic fieldwork conducted in various highland villages of Kayseri, Turkey, the paper asks how migrant men come to terms with this challenge.

Extant literature on migration addresses the gendered nature of remittance houses by asking how the practice of building a house is a male performance that enables migrant men to retain their status in the homeland. The house serves a central role in the performance of masculinity. The annual trips to the homeland, which usually involve the entire family, and month-long stays in the remittance house, serve as a reminder to the rest of the community that migrant men in general, and fathers, in particular, are still in charge of their families and continue to serve as the heads of their households. Building a remittance house becomes a performance that is central to uniting the family together under one roof and bringing Europe-born children back to the homeland.

This function, however, is being challenged. Rather than serving as empowering symbols of masculinity, remittance houses transform into emasculating structures. The remittance house starts to serve a function that undermines men's role in the community and status in the eyes of others. My paper shows that empty remittance houses, particularly those that are not visited annually by migrants, as well as those which are

not visited by the Europe-born second generation children generate gossip about the potential hardships a household faces in the host country, as well as potential hardships of keeping the family together—both of which are interpreted as weaknesses on migrant men and their fulfillment of the role as the heads of their households.
***

A Geographical Assesment on Human Smuggling Accross Turkey

(7) Arife Karadağ (Ege University)

Recently, Turkey has increasingly been the scene of illegal border crossings and human smuggling due to its location that is convenient for transit among the continents of Asia, Europe and Africa, the advantageous (!) condition offered by its geography for the transits via its borders, and the still ongoing political, economic and strategic instabilities in its border neighbors. The present study deals with human smuggling that we may regard as another side of trade on our borders and it aims to make geographical evaluations about the illegal migration and human smuggling movements, which have obviously increased recently on the borders of Turkey that is located on the route of transit migration at international level and which form some sort of threat with their socio-economic and security dimensions on our borders, within the scope of crime geography.

***

Review of Irregularity in Remittances

(30TP) Ibrahim Sirkeci (Regent's University London), Fethiye Tilbe[1] (Namık Kemal University/Regent's University London) and Therese Svensson (Regent's University London)

According to the World Bank, by October 2014, total remittance flows reached USD 582 billion, which is about three times the size of global official aid and nearly as large as total foreign direct investments. Nevertheless, these estimates are likely to represent only a portion of the total remittances volume. Since a significant but unknown volume of funds find their way through informal channels. Migrant workers often use both formal and informal money transfer methods for various reasons. Irregular migration status is an important reason among others.

Informal remittance systems (IRS) have been in place probably since the first ever human migration but known by different names. Key operational characteristics as mentioned in the literature that make IRS so successful are the

1 Araştırmacı bu çalışmayı TÜBİTAK, 2214/A-Yurt Dışı Doktora Sırası Araştırma Burs Programı kapsamında gerçekleştirmiştir.

speed and efficiency, accessibility and affordability, cultural practices and preferences, and relational contracts. Informal remittance systems are attractive to certain users due to simplicity, efficiency, low cost and/or reliability. Nevertheless, it comes with risks and uncertainty because of (often) undocumented/unregistered nature of these transactions.

In this study, we review literature on informal migrant remittance channels to identify gaps and future research avenues in the field. There is a limited literature on IRS and the existing studies are often vague and with contradictory arguments about the ways in which IRS operates.
***

SESSION 2C – Göç ve Sürgün Edebiyatı

Sibirya'dan Sürgün Edilen Bir Şair: Anempodist İvanoviç Sofronov (Alampa) ve Babama Mektup Şiiri

(143) Gülsüm Killi Yılmaz (Ankara University)

Saha (Yakut) Türk edebiyatının kurucularından biri olan Anempodist İvanoviç Sofronov (Alampa) (1886-1935) özellikle toplumsal içerikte kaleme aldığı oyunları, şiir ve öyküleri ile tanınmaktadır. Sofronov sadece edebiyatçı değil, aynı zamanda eleştirmen, gazeteci ve fikir adamıdır. Sofronov (Alampa) Sibirya'nın en sert iklim koşullarına sahip olan, Polonya ve Merkezi

Rusya'dan çok sayıda fikir adamı, yazar ve aydının sürgün yeri olarak tanınan bugünkü Saha Cumhuriyeti topraklarında aslında zengin bir köylünün çocuğu olarak dünyaya gelmiştir. Ailesinin yaşadığı bazı talihsizlikler sonucu oldukça zor bir çocukluk geçirmiş, öğrenim hayatını sürdürememiş, ancak tüm yaşadığı güçlükler ve vatanına duyduğu sevgi onu vatanının kaderi konusunda daha çok düşünmeye ve çalışmaya itmiştir. Böylece 1912-1913 yıllarında "Golos Yakuta (Yakut'un Sesi)" gazetesinde yazdığı şiirleriyle yayın hayatına başlamış, bir taraftan Çarlık karşıtı bir tavırla yayın hayatını sürdürürken toplumsal ve politik hareketlere liderlik etmiştir. Sofronov, 1927 yılında "konfederalist harekete katılmak ve burjuvazi ulusçuluğu yapmak" suçlamaları ile Rusya'nın Avrupa kısmında kalan Arhangelsk bölgesine sürülmüştür. Sofronov'un 1934 yılında ağırlaşan tüberküloz hastalığıyla son bulan sürgün hayatında kaleme aldığı "Ağabar Suruk (Babama Mektup)" adlı eseri, şairin çok sevdiği vatanına duyduğu özlemi, haksızca sürgün edilmesine karşı duyduğu isyanı ve sevdiklerinden ayrılmanın verdiği hüznü en canlı biçimde yansıtan eserlerinden biridir. Bu bildiride "Babama Mektup" eserinden yola çıkılarak, yaşadığı ve sevdiği topraklardan, sevdiklerinden koparılan sanatçının duygu dünyasının şiirine yansımaları ele alınacaktır.

***

Bir Kıyamet Provası: Göçe Sürgün Hayatlar

(105) Mevhibe Coşar (Karadeniz Teknik Üniversity)

Taşların yerinden oynaması, dağların yerinden oynamasıdır; dağların yerinden oynaması da kıyamet(1). Sözlükler kıyameti, "Dünyanın yıkılıp harap olması; her şeyin mahvolması; dünyanın sonu ve mahşer meydanına bütün insanların dirilip toplanacağı zaman" olarak tanımlıyor. Bir Trabzon türküsü, "Trabzon'dan çıktım koptu kıyamet" sözleriyle başlarken taşların yerinden oynamasını, vatandan ayrılışın derin ızdırabından hareketle insanın ezeli ve ebedi acısını, bir ney'in kamışlıktan koparılışındaki inleyişini yeniden dile getiriyor. İnsanın hikâyesi zaten tam da ayrılığın kapısında başlıyor: vatandan, yardan, hayattan... Sonra insan dönüp bu hikâyeyi anlatıyor ve adına edebiyat diyor. Cennetten çıkarılışından itibaren göç hâlidir insanın hâli, göçe sürgün olmak kaderi ve hikâyesinin ana temi. Ayrılığın sürgün kokulusu olan göç, bir yıkım, bir yangındır. Bu yıkım ve yangının insana söylettikleri ise göçün hikayesidir. 1 Kasım 1914, bir oldubitti ile savaşa giren Osmanlı topraklarına Rusların girdiği tarihtir. Karadeniz'de ilerleyişini sürdürürken 8 Martta Rize'ye çıkan Rus askerleri, 30 Martta Sürmene'yi işgal etmişti. Bu tarihler itibariyle Karadeniz halkının batıya amansız göçü başlar. Hayatlarının en uzun iki yılını geçirmek, "dönmek" hayali ile "gitmek", yerini yurdunu terk etmek zorunda kalan Trabzon halkı, "yol" boyunca "açlık" ve "salgın hastalıklarla" "mücadele" etti, bir çoğu yollarda öldü. Onlardan geriye anılar kaldı (2), yanık türküler ve destanlar. Bu çalışmada yerelden ulusala ve oradan evrensele uzanmak üzere, savaş ve işgal merkezinde Trabzon halkının "sürgün" duygusu ile "kıyamet" tasvirine dayandırdığı muhacirliği, sözlü edebiyat ürünleri üzerinden anlamak ve anlatmak amaçlanmıştır. Bu amaç doğrultusunda söz konusu dönemde üretilen, kısmen musikinin eşlik ettiği türkü, destan ve anlatılar değerlendirilecektir. Böylece "göç"ün kelimeleri, bu kelimeler aracılığı ile de insan algısında "göç"ün konumlandırılışı ortaya konulmaya çalışılacaktır.

***

Language and Identity Perception in Nazım Hikmet's Poetry during Exile Years

(97) Hülya Bayrak Akyıldız (Anadolu University)

This paper aims to examine Nazım Hikmet's poetry during his years of exile, in terms of language and identity perception. These two may seem irrelevant but the fact is they are strongly related as the poet's forced to perceive both the language and his national identity in a foreign surrounding that put him in a position of independent observer. This surrounding made the poet to leave his comfort zone and see the richness and failures of both. The poet makes a lot of comparisons of culture in his poems. He can be critical towards his own culture while idealising it at the same time. He misses his country and his family and he tends to overidealise the land where his roots lay. He accentuates his bonds with his country and nationality more than any other Turkish poet or writer. He never wrote a verse other than in Turkish but he wasn't published in Turkish those days. He neither had a passport nor a citizenship of Turkey but he represented Turkey in some international organizations such as Asian African Writers Union, carrying his language and recognition as a Turkish poet as a passport. I would like to point out this accentuation in his work during the exile years.

***

Sürgünün Getirdikleri: Yezidin Kızı – Sürgün – Nilgün Romanlarında Göç ve Sürgünün İzleri

(126) Yakup Çelik (Yıldız Teknik University)

Refik Halit Karay'ın 1923 sonrasında 150'likler arasında sürgüne gönderilmesinden sonra kaleme aldığı ve bu yılların seyahat ve zorunlu göç izlenimlerinin ürünü olan üç romanında acıyla bütünleşmiş insan manzaraları, yok olan hayatlar ve özellikle genç kızların drama dönüşmüş yaşamaları işlenmektedir. Bir prensesin bovarizmin de izlerini taşıyan sürgündeki hayatının anlatıldığı Nilgün romanında, çöken bir imparatorluğun bakiyesi durumundaki insanların drama dönüşmüş yaşama biçimleri; Sürgün'de, zorunlu göçün parçaladığı hatta yok ettiği bir aile; Yezidin Kızı'nda da bir azınlık mensubu genç kızın sürekli göçler ve sürgünlerle şekillenmiş drama dönüşmüş hayatı söz konusu edilmektedir.

Bildirimizde bu üç roman çevresinde Refik Halit Karay'ın insanlık dramı olarak kabul edilen göç ve sürgüne nasıl baktığı, özellikle genç kızların bu olaylardan nasıl etkilendiği üzerinde durulacaktır.

***

Onlar da İnsandı: Acar Cengiz Dağcı ve Kasimali Bayalinov'un İzinde Zorunlu Göçlerle Sürgün Edilmiş Hayatlar"

(141) Figen Günerdilek (Gazi University)

Bu bildiride, kendisi de Stalin Rusyası'nda sürgüne mahkum edilen Kırım Türkü Cengiz Dağcı'nın Onlar da İnsandı eseri ve Çarlık Rusyasında kendisi de Çin'e sürgün edilen Kırgız Türkü Kasımalı Bayalinov'un "Acar" adlı romanlarının izinde zorunlu bir göç olarak sürgün konusu irdelenecektir.

"Onlar da İnsandı" adlı eserde, 1928 ve 1932 yıllarında Kırım topraklarında, Kızıltaş köyü örneğinde Rusların istila yoluyla Kırım Türklerinin topraklarını ele geçirmelerinin ve toprağın asıl sahiplerini kendi topraklarında sürgün/göçmen durumuna düşmelerinin hikayesi anlatılır. Acar adlı eserde ise Çin'e zorunlu olarak göç etmiş sürgün bir Kırgız kızı "Acar" ile 1916 yılında Kırgız halkının bu zorunlu göç yani "ürkün" sırasındaki ve sonrasındaki zor hayatı anlatılır.

Bu eserler; iki farklı coğrafyada iki farklı Türk boyunun iki farklı Rus yönetimi sürecinde maruz kaldıkları iki sürgün hikayesinin benzer uygulamaları, benzer sonuçları ve benzer insan hikayeleri ortaya çıkarması bakımından önemlidir. Yazarlarının anlattıkları bu hikayelerde geçen olaylara dair bizzat yaşanmışlıklarının olması ayrıca ilgi çekicidir.

Bildirimizde, bir açıdan iç göç, bir açıdan da dış göç sayılabilecek sürgünler ve kurbanları adı geçen eserlerde karşılaştırmalı ve tarihî olarak incelenecektir.

***

SESSION 2D – Migrant Identity

Towards The Signs of Turkish Ethnic Identity in a Midsize Norwegian City

(4) Karolina Nikielska-Sekula (Telemark University College)

This paper, employing visual methods of sociology (Krase 2012) and situational analysis

(Clarke 2005) focuses on a visible presence of inhabitants of Turkish origin in a midsize city situated in the western part of Norway. In 2013, 25% of the city's inhabitants had an immigrant background (SSB 2014) with the majority (13.5%) being of Turkish origin (ibidem). Most of them arrived to the city as "guest workers" in the late 1960s and 1970s and were followed afterwards by other members of their families. Due to their prolonged length of stay they have managed to make an imprint on the city by their visible presence in Drammen influencing practices of ethnic Norwegian inhabitants. The aim of this paper is to present how immigrants of Turkish origin use the buildings in the city adjusting them to multiple facilities from cultural and religious associations to commercial services such as restaurants and groceries. Meaning and functions of the new spaces will be analyzed.

The study shows that immigrants of Turkish origin indeed have changed the meaning of the inner-city space adapting resources in new localities to their needs (Krase 2012: 18). They have designed Turkish-styled spaces within Norwegian-styled buildings including churches, changing the sense of the space. It has been observed that practices of inhabitants with Turkish background go beyond the limits of what was formerly assumed as mere ethnic habits, even if their sense of "turkishness" remains very strong. A tendency to involve signs of Norwegian ethnic

identity into a creation of new, multicultural and transnational spaces was observed.
***

Identity building in youth cultures

(114) Manfred Zentner (Danube University Krems)

Nowadays youth and young adults have many opportunities but also face a great many of challenges when growing up since in times of globalisation and individualisation everyone can time choose the models from various cultural influences but at the sameis responsible of creating his/her own identities. Patchwork identities and self expression in consumer societies are results of this development. These challenges hold for all youth in Europe, but those young migrants of the 2nd genration have to find their place in the host society as well as in the tradition of their families, they have to accept both the value system in the host society and their traditions. Global youth cultures and scenes can serve as sources for values and attitudes as well as cultural heritage, traditions and religions or ideologies.

This paper focuses on the approaches of youth with Turkish background in Austria in their identity building in youth cultures, especially in the fitness, house, soccer and hiphop scene. Young men and women describe in qualitative interviews their youth cultures and explain why they are in this certain youth culture in Austria, what they are looking for and what challenges they face in these scenes because of having a Turkish background. Especially the reactions of families and peers regarding either acceptance and support or disagreement of the youth cultures are reflected.

***

The Multidimensionality of Migration

(117) Ayşenur Talat Zrilli (Middle East Technical University)

The multidimensionality of migration, although often acknowledged, is a rather neglected issue in mainstream migration theorizing. On the one hand, migration theories often focus on labour migrations, and on the other hand, they overemphasize either macro-level economic-structural or micro-level economic-rational causal factors at the expense of cultural, political or ideational ones. This paper has the immigrations from Turkey to North Cyprus between 1975-1979 (the first wave of migrations from Turkey to North Cyprus) as its empirical focus. This case, though under-researched, is rather well suited to conceptualize the causal complexity, multi-dimensionality and multi-factoriality of the phenomenon of migration. The beginnings of the emergence of a migration system between Turkey

and North Cyprus dates back to the division of the island following inter-ethnic clashes between Greek and Turkish Cypriots, and the foundation of an ethnically homogeneous state in the northern part of the island in 1975. The immigration of a relatively large number of Turkish nationals was facilitated by the states of Turkey and North Cyprus and involved the settlement of mostly farmer families from Anatolia to the villages in the northern part of Cyprus evacuated by Greek Cypriots. Yet, even though the movement is officially referred to as a case of labour migration, a causal analysis reveals the interaction of not only economic-structural but also political and cultural factors within the migration generating mechanisms. Data was collected from experts - bureaucrats and politicians- and from immigrants via qualitative methods -participant observation, semi-structured in depth interviews and oral history interviews. A critical realist meta-theoretical framework informs this study, which is also especially useful in highlighting the multidimensionality of the concept of migration.
***

Learning Germanness: Integration Courses and Negotiated Identities of Turkish Immigrants in Germany

(46) Daniel Williams (Carleton College)

Since 2000, Germany has officially moved away from a national self-understanding as a from a "non-immigration" country that privileges descent-based citizenship and ethnicity, to a more "civic" nation that recognizes the permanent presence and potential inclusion of immigrants and their children. This has been expressed most clearly in a new Nationality Act passed in 2000, which created territorial birthplace citizenship (*jus soli*) for the first time in modern German history. Another site of this change came in 2006, when the first ever Integration Program was institutionalized. The main components of this program are mandatory language and "civics" courses for new immigrants to Germany. The importance of such courses is reflected not only in their mandatory completion for certain groups of immigrants. In this paper, I examine how these courses become sites for constructing Germanness / foreignness as well as Germany as a nation. I examine these constructions in two ways. First, I analyze and explore the *content and curriculum* of these courses, as knowledge about Germany. I especially focus on how this knowledge is "organized" and represented. Second, I use ethnographic methods—both observation of integration classes and interviews with immigrants who participate in integration courses, and consider how they construct Germany, Germanness, and their own identities. My interviewee sample focuses especially on Turkish immigrants, with some other nationalities represented for comparative purposes. The analysis sheds light not only on the variety of meanings of Germanness in the "new" Germany, but also on questions of how immigrants' view national identity—their own and that of others.

***

SESSION 3A – Integration, Harmonization, Marginalization

A Comparative Study of Turkish Migrants in Germany, France and Switzerland

(78) Ali Çağlar (Hacettepe University)

The main aim of this study is to investigate and discuss the problems of the Turkish origin migrants faced and experienced in Germany, France and Switzerland. To achieve the aim, firstly, the Turkish origin groups – associations - organized in these countries are determined, and all groups are included. Secondly, the presidents of their associations, the people who are accepted as the public opinion leaders who are influential on their communities, the political people who have Turkish origin, and business and trades people are determined. It is thought that these people are best observers, and the people who are aware of the problems faced and experienced by their community members. In total, 106 semi-structured interviews and focus groups (52 in

Germany, 32 in Switzerland and 52 in France) are carried out to get the data needed. In these presentation, it is mostly focused on their identity perceptions, problems they faced and the relationships between them. It is also seen that the problems faced and experienced are more or less the same although each group put itself in a different place and define differently.

***

Post-Immigration Policies in Turkey: Integration versus Harmonization

(87) Gülay Uğur Göksel (Istanbul Aydın University)

Immigration is a process not a static phenomenon. It has been happening from the beginning of time for variety of reasons. As the reasons and the consequences of immigration have been studied vigorously by disciplines, we come to an understanding that politics of immigration necessitates multilayered and interdisciplinary approach. On the other hand, the politics of immigration in Turkey is a relatively new phenomenon which social scientists are still try to grasp the implications of immigration to the specific case of Turkey. When we look at the official discourse on immigration and Turkish immigration literature, many arguments on the integration of immigrants are riddled with contradictions. One of the basic problems is the ambivalent

approach to the issue of integration of Syrian refugees into the Turkish societies. Syrian refugee flow is one of the biggest rapid immigration flows in the world history. In this paper, I want to investigate post-immigration policies of Turkey. Managing Syrian refugee crisis was an important test for the newly established Directorate General of Migration Management. But, how is the integration of this massive amount of refugees imagined? The official discourse refers to the integration process as harmonization. What are the reasons behind this discursive change? How can harmonization be achieved? What kid of political and social change is necessary? Asking questions on immigrant integration also means asking questions about the inner dynamics of the host country itself. So, these questions will eventually make us question the ethnic and religious identities in Turkish society.
***

The Notion of Integration and Economic Aspects in the German Discourse of a Culturally Sensitive Elderly Care

(142) Nevin Altıntop (University of Vienna)

German-wide the paradigm of Intercultural Opening is presented as consensus with respect to inclusion and integration of migrants. Its theoretical discourse highlights ethical standards as well as quality and progress in health care. As a

result, culturally sensitive health care solutions became fashionable in all their rhetoric and substantial nuances from intercultural to transcultural or culturally specific. My contribution presents an analysis of a field research on culturally sensitive elderly care focused on Turkish migrants in Germany. It contrasts the patterns of the theoretical debates with actual health care situations provided by different welfare organizations and private investors covering ambulant as well as stationary care units. The results reveal the weakness and vulnerability of culturally sensitive health care solutions when they encounter economic decisions that are oriented on profit: a culturally specific or sensitive elderly care is regarded as niche in market or for project funding. Elder migrants are the new clients within the elderly care sector who, finally, have to accept specific health care solutions. In conclusion, the actual situation of a culturally sensitive health care in Germany takes a delicate balance between inclusion and marginalization of elderly migrants.
***

First generation Turkish migrants in the Netherlands: strong ties between region of origin and place of residence

(85) Han Nicolaas (Statistics Netherlands) and Farhana Rahman (Bangladesh Women's Health Coalitions (BWHC))

The number of first generation Turkish migrants in the Netherlands amounted to almost 200 thousand on 1 January 2014. Many of them came in the late 1950s and the 1960s to the Netherlands and other western European countries as so-called 'guest workers'. The second wave consisted of family reunion migrants (spouses and children) who joined their husbands of the first wave of labour migration. After a while, family formation caused a rise in immigration: as single Turkish men started to realise that their stay in the Netherlands would be much longer than originally intended, or even permanent, they decided to find a partner in their native countries.

A majority of these first generation Turkish migrants have their roots in rural areas in Turkey, especially Central- and Eastern Anatolia.

Turkish migrants, like many other immigrant groups, tend to live in the neighbourhood of their compatriots. By combining the places of birth of first generation Turkish migrants to their current destination in the Netherlands it becomes clear that strong ties exist between the region of origin of Turkish migrants and their place of residence in the Netherlands.

The very first immigrants who settled in the Netherlands took care of housing facilities and often arranged a job for family members, fellow-villagers and fellow countrymen. This so-called chain migration strengthened the ties with the region of origin. Therefore, Turkish immigrants in certain Dutch municipalities originate from a limited number of regions in Turkey.

In this paper, we not only analyse the relationship between region of origin and place of destination of Turkish immigrants. We also look at the relationship between region of origin and period and age of arrival in the Netherlands as well as fertility of Turkish women in the Netherlands by region of origin.

***

SESSION 3B – Family Formation and Migration

The Fear of "What They Say": How Gossip Regulates Sexual Exploration among Migrants in Europe

(115) Sherria Ayuandini (Washington University in St. Louis) and Oğuz Alyanak (Washington University in St. Louis)

Gossip has long been recognized as an effective controlling mechanism of one's behavior. The fear of "what they say" is an important factor that shapes one's engagement in urban life and participation in leisure practices. Among Muslims in Europe, evading gossip becomes an important part of everyday life. It requires a careful effort to keep secrets undisclosed. In this paper, we focus on Turks in the Netherlands and

France and ask how they deal with gossip on an everyday basis. We provide ethnographic snapshots of the ways that Muslim Turks in general, and the youth in particular, invent ways to navigate social norms that regulate appropriate sexual practice.

In the Netherlands, we focus on discussions on virginity among Muslim Turks in Amsterdam. In a context in which virginity is still seen as an important aspect of an unmarried person's life, gossip and rumor are often the direct driving forces that inform and shape decisions of intimacy and partner choice. Women of Turkish descent are still largely expected to be sexually untouched before marriage. A gossip that insinuates otherwise has proven to significantly affect a young woman's life unfavorably. What do young Turkish women in Amsterdam do to cope with gossip over their sexual life?

In France, we focus on Turkish men's sexual explorations in Strasbourg. As a border-town, Strasbourg provides easy access to Germany where brothels and casinos are conveniently located. Although men are ascribed the role of (future-) fathers who would attend to their family and kin, living in this hyper-sexualized geography brings the possibility of having affairs with sex workers—which makes crossing the border into Germany a suspicious act in itself. The blame for increasing rates of divorce among Muslim Turks in France are sought after men's cross-border

excursion which puts men under the spotlight. What do Turkish men in Strasbourg do to evade gossip over their cross-border excursions?
***

Changing Patterns of Migration through Marriage: A Case Study of the Route from Konya to North Europe

(93) Besim Can Zırh (Middle East Technical University) and Didem Yıldırım (Middle East Technical University)

The 50th anniversary of the guest-worker agreement between Turkey and Germany was celebrated in 2011. It is not possible to understand this half-century period as homogenous and uniform. Family reunification and transnational marriages appeared as a specific form of migration in the wake of the labour migration halt in 1974 and continued until today in tandem with increasing concerns by policy-makers of receiving-countries. However, the issue of changing patters of migration through marriage in this period has not been problematized in relation to changing social and economic contexts. Our paper, based on primary research conducted during the summer 2014, attempts to focus on this issue in the case of migration from Konya to North European countries such as Norway and Sweden. In other words, our paper aims discover changing characteristics of "migration through marriage" which can be explained as "marrying with a person who holds a foreign citizenship in order to migrate." Within the framework of our research, we conducted (a) in-depth interviews with migrant and non-migrant members of extended families, senior citizens, shopkeepers and local authorities and (b) participated in marriage ceremonies in three sending-districts (Beyşehir, Cinahbeyli and Kulu) in Konya. We suggest understanding this specific form of migration by specifying five different patterns evolved in the last 40 years in accordance to changing context of migration. Although it is true that marriage bounds still reinforce transnational relations between sending and receiving countries, it is also interesting to note that neither migrant nor non-migrant families do prefer their children to marry transnationally since the early-2000s.

***

Wars and Brides

(46TP) Dilek Cindoğlu (Mardin Artuklu University)

This paper is meta analysis on the relationship between wars and women's bodies by looking at a newly rising phenomenon of "cross-border brides" between Syria and Turkey after the breakout of the Syrian Civil War. Although the Middle Eastern societies falls short on gender equality measures in general, precarious times like civil wars worsen the local oppressive gendered processes by adding further new burdens on women and young girls. The rising literature on the "Arab Spring" mainly focuses on the civil-military relations and democratic transition in the global context. This paper, on the other hand, focuses on the ways in which wars weaken women and place them in even more precarious positions by reducing their bodies and sexualities to a commodity. The on-line sites, newspaper stories and local narratives provide ample data for the nature of these inequalities and oppressions in these "cross-border" arranged marriages; between young Syrian girls and older men of Turkey mostly as a second co-wives. In short, this paper will be discussing the gendered impacts of wars in the precarious times in general, Syrian Civil war in particular by looking at the "cross-border marriages" after the breakout of the Syrian Civil War.

***

SESSION 3C – Göç ve Uyum

İç Göçün Sosyal Dışlanma Boyutunda İncelenmesi Manisa İli Alan Araştırması

(155) Ramazan Temel (Manisa Celal Bayar University) and Hülya Yeşilyurt Temel (Manisa Celal Bayar University)

Coğrafi mekân değişikliğiyle sosyal, ekonomik, kültürel ve siyasi boyutta toplum yapısında değişliğe neden olan nüfus hareketliliği olarak tanımlanan göç olgusu, aslında insanlık tarihi kadar eski bir olgudur. Tarih boyunca insanların daha iyi ve yeni bir yaşam kalitesini kendilerine ve ailelerine sağlama istekleri, göçün küreselleşme ile birlikte son 20-30 yılda farklı bir görünüm kazanmasına neden olmuştur.

Türkiye'de ilk zamanlar yoğun olarak görülmeyen iç göç hareketleri, 1950'li yıllarda toplumu derinden etkileyen bir olgu halini almıştır. Yaşanan tarımsal dönüşümün kentin çekiciliği karşısında yetersiz kalması, iç göçlerin yoğun bir şekilde yaşanmasına yol açmıştır. Özellikle 2011 yılından itibaren ülkemize gelen Suriyeli ve Iraklı sığınmacıların da artması göç olgusunun "kavram" niteliğinden çıkıp "insani boyut" kazandığını gösterir niteliktedir. Bu bağlamda, gerek iç gerekse dış göç aslında göç eden bireyleri göç ettikleri yerlerde birçok sorunla karşı karşıya bırakmaktadır. Bunlar yoksulluk, kentsel yoksulluk, gecekondulaşma, iş piyasasında yer bulamama, eğitim-sağlık ve ulaşım gibi temel ihtiyaçlara erişememe, kayıt dışı istihdama yönelme gibi sorunların yanında göç eden bireylerin karşılaştığı en önemli sorun ve çalışmanın ana teması olan sosyal dışlanmadır.

Sosyal dışlanma kavramı yeni olmamakla birlikte çok sayıda ve farklı tanımları mevcuttur. Sosyal dışlanma; kişinin topluma uyumunu sağlayan sosyal, ekonomik, politik ve kültürel sistemden kısmen veya tamamen dışlayan bir süreç olarak tanımlanmıştır. Sosyal dışlanma içinde ele alınan gruplar arasında göçmenler önemli bir yer tutmaktadır. Göçmenlerin göç ettikleri toplumlarda yaşadıkları dışlanma daha çok ekonomik, kültürel, sosyal ve siyasal farklılıklardan kaynaklanmaktadır.

Bu çalışmada Ege Bölgesi'nde tarım ve sanayi şehirlerinden olan Manisa ilinde, göçle gelen Doğulu ve Güneydoğulu göçmenlerin yanında, ilçe ve köylerden göç eden bireylerin sosyal dışlanma boyutu incelenmiştir. Çalışmada göç eden yirmi beş kişiyle yarı yapılandırılmış araştırma yöntemlerinden mülakat tekniği kullanılmıştır. Görüşmeler sırasında göçmenlere göç nedenleri, göç hikâyeleri ve Manisa'ya geldikten sonra yaşadıkları sorunlara ilişkin sorular yöneltilmiştir. Soruların odak noktası göçmenlerin sosyal dışlanma deneyimleme biçimlerine maruz kalıp/kalmadıklarıdır.
***

Bir Küresel Kamu Malı Olarak Mülteci Sorunu

(17TP) Birol Kovancılar (Manisa Celal Bayar University)

Göç ve mülteci sorunu önemi artan ve ülkelerin gündeminde giderek üst sıralara tırmanan sadece ulusal boyuttan ziyade bunun ötesinde küresel boyutta bir sorun durumundadır. Ulusal boyutların ötesinde, bölgesel ve daha çok küresel boyutta etki ve sonuçlara sahiptir. Ayrıca sorunun doğasının küresel özellikler göstermesine rağmen finansman ve sorunun çözümü açısından ülkelerin üzerinde uzlaştıkları yaygın kabul görmüş çözüm veya yöntemler geliştirilemediği gözlenmektedir. Dolayısıyla çalışmamız mülteci sorununu küresel boyutta ele alacak ve küresel kamu malları teorisi çerçevesinde inceleyecek, finansmanı için alternatif yöntem ve yük paylaşım önerileri ortaya koymaya çalışacaktır.

***

Mahalli Yönetimlerde Yabancılar: Sorunlar ve Çözüm Önerileri

(29TP) Mustafa Ökmen (Manisa Celal Bayar University) and Güven Şeker (Manisa Celal Bayar University)

Yerel yönetimler hizmet sunmak için görev yapan birimleridir. Sunulan hizmetler ulusal mevzuatların gereği olduğu kadar küresel hale gelen dünyada herkes tarafından beklen(ebilecek)en faaliyetler olarak ortaya çıkmaktadır.

İnsanlar yerleşik yaşadıkları kadar bu gün artık hareketli bir halde farklı yerlerde hayatlarını devam ettirebilmektedirler. İnsanlar yeni geldikleri yere emek, sermaye ve birikim getirmektedirler, bu değerlerin geldiği yerde de yaşamlarını menşe yerlerinde sürdürdüklerine benzer istendik şekilde geçirebilmek için hizmet beklerler. Türkiye küreselleşme, sermayenin ülkeye çekilmesi, uluslararası alanda yapılan sözleşme ve antlaşmaların gereği gibi etkenler ile ulusal mevzuatta farklı düzenlemeleri de gerektiğinde yaparak yerel yönetimlerde hareketli gruplara göre düzenleme yapabilmektedir.

Çalışma karşılaştırmalı olarak yerel yönetimlerin yükümlü oldukları hizmetleri yerine getirirken yerel halk dışında kalan yabancı gruplara hizmet sunumunda yaklaşımları, bu yaklaşımlardaki değişimleri ele alarak geleceğe yönelik bakış açıları ile ele alacaktır.
***

SESSION 3D – Migration Policy and Perceptions

Continuity or Change in Turkey's Migration Policy: From 1989 émigrés to Syrian "guests"

(25) N. Aslı Şirin Öner (Marmara University) and Deniz Genç (İstanbul Medipol University)

In this paper, Turkey's migration policy is examined in the case of mass migration of two groups: the ethnic Turks of Bulgaria, who migrated forcefully to Turkey in the summer of 1989 and the Syrians, who are displaced as a result of the conflict in Syria and have been forced to migrate to Turkey in large numbers since 2011. The Turkish government considered the ethnic

Turks of Bulgaria as "kindreds" while the Syrians are regarded as "guests". But more than the discourse on these groups, Syrians' mass migration has heralded to a different phase of Turkey's migration management. New Law on Foreigners and International Protection, which aims to update the country's migration regime according to the necessities of today's migration movements, has entered into force in April 2014, and the Directorate General of Migration Management with numerous bureaucrats trying to earn expertise on migration issues, has been established. Yet, the question of whether there has been a paradigmatic shift in the management of mass migrations in Turkey begs for research. In line with these, the questions that the present paper seeks answers are as follows: In the light of the approaches towards these groups, is there a continuity or change in Turkey's migration policy in the case of a mass migration? What might be the prevalent aspects of Turkey's mass migration policy? What are the similarities and differences between the approaches adopted by the government towards these groups and why are they so?
***

The Political Economy of Anti-Immigration and the Syrian Refugees in Turkey

(91) Mehmet Gökay Özerim (Yaşar University)

This study aims to analyze and discuss the hidden economic concerns behind anti-immigration stances and sentiments against Syrian refugees in Turkey by exemplifying the economic themes in anti-immigration discourse of the specific actors. Stemming from the idea of analyzing anti-immigration discourse in conjunction with the economic context of the issue, this paper purposes to outline and discover which economic and financial arguments have been asserted by anti-immigrant actors. By taking the open door immigration policy decision of Turkish government for the Syrians by 2011 and the following refugee flows as a case, the study focuses on and analyzes the discourse of the trade unions and labor unions as the specific actors of the process in the towns where the Syrian refugees are populated in Turkey. The study reveals that trade unions and labor unions are influential and active actors of the process since they directly contact with public or local labor and they develop an agenda and salience by concrete reports and meetings.
***

Coping with Mass Influxes: Turkey's Management of 1991 Iraqi and On-going Syrian Refugee Crises

(110) Zeynep Şahin Mencütek (Gediz University) and Ela Gökalp Aras (Gediz University)

This study aims to understand factors shaping the assistance structure and the policies of hosting countries in the emergency response to mass influx. In this regard, as focusing on the case of Turkey, it seeks to explore Turkey's coping strategies and policies with mass influxes, which can be seen as the important challenges and determinants of Turkey's immigration and asylum policy along with the European Union's impacts. The paper questions, which factors - including political context, legal provision, and external factors-influence the choice of response? What kinds of discourses are developed? How Turkey's policy responses can be explained with the other external forces such as the existing international norms and particularly the EU's immigration and asylum policies? How and when Turkey shares responsibility and burden with international governmental agencies like the UNHCR, IOM and non-governmental organizations? This study responds these questions by comparing two mass influx crises, namely Iraqi (1991) and the ongoing Syrian mass influxes.

First Gulf War (1990-1991) in Iraq and Civil War in Syria that has continued since March 2011 led to mass forced migration of many people who had to be internally displaced and/or to pour into neighbouring countries for seeking protection. In 1991, 460.000 Iraqis, most of them are Kurds and Turkmens- living in the Northern Iraq arrived in Turkey's border after March 1991 uprising.3 On the other hand, since the beginning of the crisis in Syria, the number of Syrian refugees in Turkey has significantly gone up.4 They are hosted in camps along the border and spread in cities. Despite similarities in Iraqi and Syrian refugee situation, Turkey adopted two different policies in the emergency response to a mass influx. It refused to allow the Kurds into the country in 1991, closed its borders to limit numbers. So, she kept them outside of Turkish territory in the "safe area/haven". Turkey searched for humanitarian assistance from international community for provision of food and tents. On the other hand, it has adopted open door policy to Syrian refugees and met their basic needs by using its own resources mainly inside of the borders, which has been changing into a "close door policy" since March 2014. In case of Iraqis, Turkey did not grant de jure refugee status; but considered them as de facto refugees. However, in case of Syrians, as following to "guests", "temporary protection" status was provided as a part of the international protection with the emphasis on 'temporality'.

This paper aims to compare two cases regarding 'mass influx' by employing securitization theory and economisation of migration as well as findings of the extant scholarship on the relationship between foreign policy and refugees. It argues that policies towards Iraqis were mainly shaped by Turkey's security concerns about its internal Kurdish issue, thus Turkey highly securitized the situation. In the Syrian case, despite many risks about security, the state avoided using security language. Instead, its foreign policy goals seeking to become more powerful regional power, its close relationship with the opposition groups in Syria, and false assumptions about the 'length of crisis' led to launch an open door policy. However, as different from Iraqi case, the response for Syria is not uniformed but highly unsettled, which will be displayed under five different breaking-points. High securitization during the Iraqi crisis generated many humanitarian problems, although the crisis lasted short. In Syrian crisis, Turkey does not have a comprehensive plan of action, despite the fact that it has relatively high absorption or response capacity. However, as different from the case of Iraqis, rather than creating buffer-zones for them, international protection is provided; but along with the problems about 'transparency'. While better living conditions were provided for the Syrians; Turkey has also failed to disarmament of armed elements and the identification, separation and internment of combatants. Overall, the paper demonstrates how internal and external factors are intertwined and generate differences in copying with the mass influx experienced by a certain country.

This study uses the method of within case comparison and process tracing. Concerning the

Iraq case mainly archival data are collected. On the other hand, the case of Syria has been still on-going and this case should have been approached with its dynamic changing character. In this framework; the secondary hand sources such as newspapers, official and informal reports of the national and international organizations, official declarations and existing academic studies are employed in order to reveal the differences and similarities of Turkey's respond to the selected mass influxes.

***

The fundamental parameters of new Turkish migration policy and management

(18TP) Ali Zafer Sağıroğlu (Yildirim Beyazit University)

Turkey has a "sui generis" position in regard of migration. Its geopolitical position in the directions of "south- north" and "east – west" makes it an important "transit" country. On the other hand, Turkey has been "sending" considerable number of people outside the country for a long time. Throughout the history, it has also become the migrant "receiving" country. The stable policies and relative developments in its economics in last years make Turkey much more attractive for the migrants as the last destination. In addition, the crisis in the region forced the people to take refugee to it. The migration characteristics of

Turkey for the last century could be evaluated into three main periods. Turkey had followed a "nation-state" politics at the beginning of the republic and directed its migration policy around this matter. By the 1950's, migration became a part of development policies. On the other hand, the migration politics began to work with the relationship of Europe. Turkey assumed the legal obligations of Geneva Convention in 1951. However, it is hard to say that Turkey had had an inclusive migration politics until the 2000's. The preparation for new legislation and management began in 2007 and resulted in 2013. "The Law on Foreigners and International Protection" has come into the force on 11 April 2013. The law consists of three main parts: The first part is related with the foreigners, the second one is about the international protection and the third one is regulating a new institution, Directorate General of Migration Management (D.G.M.M.). The new law has brought an effective and strong management system by establishing necessary legal and administrative capacity. The new regulations try to find a balance between the security and human rights. It is admirable that the law is not shaped by the strict security concerns by ignoring the humanistic perspective, especially at the time coincided with a quite sizeable influx from the south borders. This paper aims to describe how the new legislation comes into being and what it brings new in the sense of migration management and politics.

***

SESSION 3E – International Migration

Reasons of internal migration and effects on socio-economic and rural space

(30) Murat Öztürk (Kırklareli University), Joost Jongerden (Wageningen University WUR) and Beşir Topaloğlu (Kadir Has University)

This paper will present the major findings of the research project "Post-1980 tendencies: reasons of internal migration and its economic and demographic effects on setllement places and rural population in Turkey". This research focused on the employment-migration relationship, but in doing so engeged with multiple issues, such as the process of migration, settlement in the city, the relation of settled migrats to the rural and return-migration. Based on an analyses of date, the research supports the thesis that migration is not so much about a "movement from one place to another", the classiccal migration definition, and more about a couple of movements between places in time. Relatedly, migration and counter-migration are conceptualized as part of multi-place living strategies, a simultanious engagement with urban wage labour and farming. These multi-place living structures

are re-shaping village life, among others expressed in a changing village demography. This research furthermore suggests that middle size villages in particular are loosing population, while villages in urban finger are becoming a part of cities because of both a growth of village popualtion and an expansion of the city. Data in this research have been collected in 2013 by means of qualitative and quantitative methods. These methods included a total of 25 focus group in differen 19 cities, 436 interviews with rural household members in different 74 villages, 410 interviews with members of households that migrated to the city in the last twenty years, and statistical analysis.
***

The Impact of Internal Migration on Crime

(86) Aysegül Kayaoğlu Yılmaz (Istanbul Technical University)

Internal migration is a crucial contributor to the population dynamics in Turkey. According to 2010 population census, nearly 7 percent of the population migrates across provinces between 2009 and 2010. This number is, of course, much higher when we consider longer time horizons. This enormous internal population movement leads an important portion of the population to reside in provinces different than the ones they were born. The 2009 Population census reveals that nearly 38% of the population lives in a province different than their birth place. This proportion is 83.3% for Istanbul and 66.6% for Ankara.

According to Aksit (1988), internal migration in Turkey can be analyzed in three sub-periods: before 1950; migration flows from 1950 to 1985 and the period after 1985. The first period comprise of migrations from rural to urban areas. Impact of *1934 Settlement Law* is undeniable for internal migration flows in this period. Second period consists of migration not only from rural to urban areas but also from urban to urban areas. Besides, internal migration has reached at very high levels in this period and these flows can be explained mainly by pull factors such as wide wage gaps across regions and employment opportunities in urban cities due to industrial clustering in those regions. The last period of internal migration is a special time span in the sense that it also includes forced migrations from rural areas of South-eastern Anatolia to the cities mainly in western part of the country together with mass migration flows due to rapid urbanization. During 1990s, there was transit migration inside Turkey because forced migrants first moved from rural areas to near-by urban centres and then migrated to larger industrialized cities. Istanbul, Ankara, Mersin and Diyarbakır were among the cities that received a substantial migrant population.

These enormous population movements to urban areas are quite often associated with urban squatters, inadequate infrastructure, poverty, income inequality, child labour, crime and so on. However, increased crime rates in cities received more attention in the media and public compare to the other migration induced problems and internal migration started to be seen as a "security" issue especially after 2000. According to Justice Statistics, the numbers of public security crimes are tripled in Turkey from 2000 to 2006. The growth rate of public security for the same period is 216%, 207% and 346% for Istanbul, Ankara and Izmir, respectively. Similar to the global tendencies to link immigrants with increasing crime rates, internal migrants in Turkey and especially in big cities like Istanbul, Ankara and Izmir, are seen as potential criminals and thus the main cause of security related problems.

After the increased instability in Eastern and South-eastern regions in 1990s and the generated forced migration flows from those regions to western part of Turkey brought up discussions about regional and ethnic differences in public space. According to the results of a survey pursued by Hacettepe University Institute of Population Studies (HIPS) in 2006, the number of internally displaced people ranged from 953,680 to 1,201,000. Visibility of new migrants (usually Kurdish citizens) made them "potential criminals" in the eyes of previous habitants and those new migrants started to be seemed as a "social problem" which triggered projects such as *"return plans"* that aimed at sending those new immigrants back to their villages where they were forced to be emptied during 1990s. Return plans were supported not only by local people but also by government officials, NGOs and even European Union officials although those actors did not pay attention whether migrants themselves wanted to return back or not.

In the contemporary Turkey, there is an already accepted view in the public that the increase in the crime rates especially in recent years is mainly due to the new migrants who were forced to migrate in 1990s. This perception of the mainstream society towards linking internal migration with insecurity and mistrust among habitants in a city can result more destructive events in the long run. Therefore, analyzing both internal migration dynamics and crime trends using the recent data is of crucial importance firstly to see whether the perceptions have any point and secondly in producing remedy-type public policies. After presenting the stylized facts, this paper aims to analyse the impact of internal migration on crime rates econometrically by employing the internal migration data from 1990, 2000 and 2010 Population Censuses together with the Justice Statistics from 1990 to 2008.
***

Language Trouble Within Ethnic Households: "Never Speak Their Mother Tongue Near Children!"

(130/10TP) Yaprak Civelek (Arel University)

The main argument of this study is based on the relationship between language shift and parental preferences about speaking "mother tongue" and "government's language" within the ethnic households. Qualitative data, "Perception of mother tongue among the ethnic households in Zeytinburnu-2014", which analyze language perception, are utilized to analyze how deliberate use of Turkish language in education creates a decision-making process for the preference of speaking mother tongue within the ethnic households in Zeytinburnu.

A "discourse analysis" is employed in order to find out how ethnic parents construct the "correlation" between the state's language politics at schools and future of their children's life-long ethnic group membership. Ethnic parents, who have children attending to primary and secondary schools, are interviewed; their feelings and concerns about turning their mother tongue into a "second language" even in their houses, the recognition that their children must speak the "government's language" and the participation in a discursively planned process in order to provide an equal opportunity for their children; thus, their awareness of the "political intention" are questioned by a qualitative approach.

The result-oriented arguments, in addition to the literature consisting language shift, are also conferred with a sociological-theoretical framework including mainly Bourdieu's "habitus", and Deleuze and Guattari's "deterritorialization of language" and critics on "educational politics",and Tollefson's "language planning".

"We, Kazakh families want their children to be successful in schools and most of the parents must speak Turkish in the houses for their future." Kazakh, 42, married, high school)

["New generation must learn Turkish very well, you see, their future, just like ours has been shaped by the Turkish-medium schools" Kurdish, 37, married, high school]

The narratives openly reveal that the parents are aware of the "direction" and see that their children must speak the "government's language" and involve in a discursively planned process of the government in order to develop their future potential.

***

Erdemli: A scene of different kinds and layers of internal immigration in Turkey

(23) Ulas Bayraktar (Mersin University), Nilgün Kiper (Karadeniz Teknik University), Burak Beyhan (Mersin University), Ali Cenap Yoloğlu (Mersin University), Hakan Erkılıç (Mersin

University) and Joseph Szyliowicz (Denver University)

Erdemli is a town 35 kilometers away from the Mersin city center. Founded in 1954 as both a district center and a municipality encompassing the three former villages, Erdemli has been the stage of different kinds of internal immigration. As being one of the most important citrus fruit producers as well as an important land for banana and vegetable greenhouses, the town hosts seasonal farm workers. Thanks to its location by the sea, she has been also a site of attraction of secondary houses that have risen all along the coast and has thus become one of the most popular destinations for seasonal domestic tourists particularly from central and southeastern Anatolia. The construction investments launched initially for such secondary summer houses have been multiplied with the conurbanisation of the Mersin metropolitan area. The town has thus welcomed new populations both as workers in these constructions and also residents of the finished buildings. In short, Erdemli is an ideal place to examine and compare different kinds of internal immigration in Turkey visible with both urban and rural characteristics.

In the framework of a TUBİTAK research project, we have been examining the socio-economic and political change in this Mediterranean town. What we propose to present in this year's Turkish Immigration Conference is to share and discuss our findings on the quantitative and qualitative aspects of the demographic change in the town.

***

SESSION 4A – Return Movements

Understanding the role of health matters in return migration: Why do elderly, chronically ill Bosnians return migrate?

(10) Line Neerup Handlos (University of Copenhagen)

In the 1990s more than 17,000 Bosnians fled the war on the Balkans and migrated to Denmark. Out of those, 2,133 have now returned to Bosnia and Herzegovina, and more are expected to follow. It has been found that return migration is especially common among the chronically ill and elderly Bosnians. Many unanswered questions remain in connection to this tendency; why do migrants return to their country of origin when they age and become ill and what role do health matters play in connection to the decision on return migration? Knowledge on drivers behind return migration among chronically ill and elderly individuals is very limited. The objective of this project was to fill this knowledge gap by looking into the life worlds of chronically ill, elderly Bosnians who had return migrated.

Semi-structured interviews were performed with 33 chronically ill and elderly Bosnians who have returned to Bosnia and Herzegovina after having lived in Denmark. All interviews were carried out in the homes of the interviewees during fieldwork in Bosnia and Herzegovina. The fieldwork took place during winter and spring 2013/2014. A Danish/Bosnian interpreter was used in all interviews and the interviews lasted between 45 minutes and 3 hours. All interviews were transcribed verbatim and translated into Danish.

When the decision on return migration was made, themes such as children and family ties in general, need for assistance in old age, nostalgia, economic incentives and wishing to die in Bosnia and Herzegovina occurred, whereas issues directly related to the chronic illness and physical health status did not seem to be prioritized.

Many factors play a role in why chronically ill and elderly Bosnians return migrate and many of these factors seem to be more important than physical health status and access to treatment of chronic illness.

***

Migrants from a Western Anatolian mountain village

(63) Gabriele Rasuly-Paleczek (University of Vienna)

This paper will present findings of an ongoing research on the links between a Western Anatolian mountain village (province of Bursa) and the outside world. Revisiting the community after nearly three decades I was struck by the enormous changes that had taken place. While most of the fields are untended and many of the former farmsteads are crumbling and only few people live permanently in the village, new houses have been constructed, garden plots fenced. In addition, contrary to past, when the village was a remote place, it is now connected by a shuttle bus and modern communication facilities and - at least from spring to fall - a constant move of people to and from the village takes place. Both migrants - including their children and grandchildren - and villagers take a keen interest the community. The village is seen as an important economic asset, as a place of recreation or retirement. Yet, it also constitutes an essential point of reference for individual and collective identities.

Next to highlighting the socio-economic changes that have taken place throughout the last three decades, my paper will focus on the different perceptions of villagers and migrants on village and urban life and the meaning both attach to the village.

This presentation is based on extensive field research in the village and the locations of migrants from that community conducted during the mid-1970ies and early 1980ies as well as in the summer of 2011 and 2012. Its main goal lies in refocusing on studying rural Turkey, if possible by conducting re-studies.

***

Causes of Return Migration by Turks from Western Europe

(64) Filiz Künüroğlu (Tilburg University), Kutlay Yağmur (Tilburg University), Fons Van De Vijver (Tilburg University) and Sjaak Kroon (Tilburg University)

We addressed return migration motivations of Turkish migrants returning from Germany, the Netherlands and France, using semi-structured oral interviews among 48 informants. Berry's acculturation model provides the conceptual background of the study. The study uses a combined qualitative and a quantitative approach to get insight into how migration and pre-return experiences, motivations and expectations of Turkish migrants influence their decisions to return to Turkey. The study revealed that motives of the returnees vary substantially across generations, genders and socio-economic status of the informants. It was found that initially determined return ambition and perceived discrimination play the most essential roles in return decisions. It is concluded that acculturation theory provides an adequate framework to interpret Turkish remigrants' experiences.

***

A Study on Relationship of Syrian Immigrants in Turkey with Their Tendency of Returning to Their Home Country

(135) Mehmet Emin Sönmez (Gaziantep University)

Majority of the immigration movement into Turkey as rest of the world is caused by random attacks, massacre, atrocity and other inhumane acts taking place in other countries. In Turkish history, as the Ottoman Empire had started to lose its territories, immigration to Anatolia gained impetus and a lot of immigrants arrived in Anatolia. The immigration movement continued during the Republic Period. For instance; Turkey received nearly one million immigrants from East Turkistan during 1950's, Afghanistan in 1982, Northern Iraq in 1988, Iraq after the Gulf War in 1991, from Bosnia between 1992 and 1998, Kosovo in 1999, and Macedonia in 2001. However, the most crowded and influential incident of immigration took place in Turkey after 2010 due to the Syrian War. The number of temporary refugees emigrating from Syria for Turkey has recently reached 2 million. Those immigrants introduced their economic, social, political and cultural problems to Turkey as well. Moreover,

there is not an established migration policy implemented by Turkey. Departing from this fact, present study was carried out to identify social, economic and cultural profile of Syrian immigrants in Turkey so that the relationship can be identified between the existing profile and their harmony with Turkey's political, cultural and economic facts, gaining and their intention to return to their home country. Study sample was selected with snowball method from many provinces. Questionnaires were used as main instrument of data collection and interviews were also used to increase validity of the study data. During analysis stage, questionnaires were analyzed with SPSS, while interviews were analyzed with qualitative analysis methods.
***

SESSION 4B – Circassian Diaspora

An Evaluation from Circassian Diaspora: The Kurdish People Example

(21TP) Bahar Ayca Okçuoğlu (Bahçeşehir University, BETAM)

Today, Circassian diaspora in Turkey has a progressive academic interest. Cultural aspects, organizations, activities, impacts on political area and future roles are topics of studies that are conducted for a long time. Conversely, the substance of precious little studies that contain of specific centers, the absence of data about relationships with other people expose that the topic still has significant deficiencies. In terms of data about diaspora and relationships with other people, this study proposes an important aim to fulfill the absence in academic area. It is also believed that this study will be an important source, for who are studying on Circassian and Kurdish movements.

This study includes the analysis of two peoples' contact point in the identity construction process of Circassian people, by using in-depth interview data of NGO representatives. Interview data are from a TUBITAK project conducted by Asst.Prof.Dr. Ulaş Sunata, titled "Diasporas in Turkey: Northwestern Caucasus People Example" (No:113K833). Even though there are a great many dimensions in the process of diasporic identity construction, the study handles to recognize the process with its one dimension, by including the references and given values specifically to Kurdish people and movement.

In the identity construction process of Circassians while giving answers to questions of 'who am I?/who are we?' and about views of current political/social issues, besides geographical and personal background difference, there are two points of view. In terms identical expressions and political claims, they consider Kurdish people and movement as an opposed entity/"other" and perform their personal/social position through this opposition. In terms of claims about education in native language and lived difficulties in first years of Republic, they create a similarity with Kurdish people's experiences and evaluate their claims rightful. As a remarkable result, they connect their potential to demand rights to provided space through Kurdish movement's progress.

***

Circassian Slavery during the Ottoman and the Republican Periods

(22TP) Elbruz Umut Aksoy (Istanbul Bilgi University)

Slavery roots are very old and deep in the Circassian culture, it goes back thousands of years and effective widely in the Circassian environments. Circassian slavery have been living in the Turkish society since the Circassian migration in 1864 and continues under different circumstances. Layout of the effects of slavery on the Circassian minority who are trying to survive in the diaspora will be discussed in this study.

Circassian Charity Association Union was established in the Second Constitutional Era in 1908. As a first mission, the Union acted for the liberation of the Ottoman Harem from Circassian slaves, the result of the negotiations the harem had been freed by subtracting 213 Circassian slaves. In October 1909, the Young Turks again received a complaint from the Union and have discussed the question of white slavery sales. At the end of discussions they prohibited the purchase and sale of the white slaves in the markets. By mistake, this decision was interpreted as the abolition of slavery in the Ottoman Empire, in fact with this article only buying and selling of slaves were prohibited and slavery had continued as a social phenomenon in the society. In addition, the Circassian slavery system unlike the classical Ottoman slave system would continue for longer time within the Circassian society.

Although the roots of Circassian slavery goes back to pre-Islamic traditions and customs of the Circassians, the slavery found its place within Sharia law and moved to the Ottoman territories with the great Circassian exile in 1864. After the collapse of the Ottoman Empire and establishment of the Turkish Republic, Circassian nobels lost their authority and control over the slave families yet illegal sales of slaves continued till the 1950s. During the 1950s the last Circassian slaves were sold.

This study will aim to focus on slaves liberation efforts and rebels against their masters during the Ottoman and Republican eras. For this purpose, the Turkification policies of the Turkish Republic in accordance with the surname regulations and its results over the slaves in the 1920s, the effects of rural-urban migration in the

1950s, and the external marriage attitudes as escape from their slavery past and afterwards will be discussed.

***

The Circassians in Turkey: From the Empire to the Nation State

(158) Caner Yelbaşı (SOAS, University of London)

The Circassians are the biggest non-Turkish ethnic groups residing in the modern Republic of Turkey after the Kurds. Their population is about 3 million. Historically, the Circassians had a unique place in Ottoman-Turkish history. During the Russian expansion into the North Caucasus in the 19th century, 90% of the indigenous Circassians – which were about a million people – were exiled to the Ottoman Empire. After their exile, which is accepted as a symbolic date on 21 May 1864, the Circassian elites were integrated and achieved significant positions in the Ottoman military and bureaucracy. Ordinary Circassians were either foot-soldier in the Ottoman military and the Hamidian Cavalry, or farmers in the regions where they were settled by the Ottomans after the exile.

With the re-institution of the Ottoman constitution of 1876 in 1908, the Circassian elites benefited from a new liberal atmosphere prevailing in the empire. They established a Circassian school and published a periodical magazine on Circassians. Later on, they were also allowed to teach the Circassian language to pupils at their own schools. However, this liberal climate did not last long period. Nearly eleven years without cessation, the empire was at war, from 1911 with the occupation of Tripolitania by Italy, the 1912-1913 Balkan Wars, the Great War between 1914-1918, up until 1919-1922 and the Turkish War of Independence. At the end of this period the Ottoman Empire collapsed, and it was replaced by a nation state, namely the Turkish Republic.

The aim of this paper is to explain how the Circassians in Turkey was affected by the transformation period of Turkey from a multicultural empire to a nation state in the early 1920s. What was the effect of this transformational process on the loyalty of Circassians towards the state and their relationship with the new Turkish Republic?
***

'Icircassia': Digital Capitalism and New Transnational Identities

(202) Lars Funch Hansen (University of Malmo)

I applied the term 'iCircassia' in my investigation of the ongoing re-territorialisation of Circassia on the Internet, which I argue constitute an addition to the usual understanding of the Circassian World as consisting of the homeland and the diaspora. This represents a new way of developing identity, including geographical-territorial identity, increasingly with the participation of long-distance actors. I use a theory by the geographer Anssi Paasi on the institutionalisation of geographical-territorial identity.

I suggest to apply the term 'digital capitalism' as an update of the terms 'print capitalism' and 'electronic capitalism' used by Benedict Anderson and Arjun Appadurai, respectively, to assign earlier periods of mediated mobilisation among ethno-national groups – with or without a nation-state. In the Circassian case this is not just exemplified by the many different Circassian websites but also by the use of social media such as Facebook, YouTube, Twitter etc., which jointly represents a new form of empowerment of Circassian actors. As such this is also a discussion of the shift experienced by the role of mediation (or mediatisation) with the arrival of Web 2.0 in this phase of late-modern globalisation, where new forms of connectivity and identity-building are developing.
***

Türkiye'deki İllerin Gelişmişlik Göstergelerinin Göç Üzerine Etkisinin İncelenmesi

(12) Sibel Selim (Celal Bayar University), Sibel
Aybarç Bursalıoğlu (Celal Bayar University),
Rıdvan Keskin (Celal Bayar University) and
Hasan Selim (Dokuz Eylül University)

Günümüzde insanlar daha rahat ortamlarda
yaşamak için genelde kırsal alanlardan şehirlere
göç etmek istemektedirler. Bu istek, kişinin göç
etmek istemesinin en önemli nedenlerinden biri-
sidir. Göçler daha çok büyük şehirlere doğru
olurken, bazen yaşanılan kırsal alanların bağlı
oldukları il ve ilçe merkezlerine, bazen de farklı
kırsal alanlara doğru olabilmektedir. Göç olayların
temelinde doğal, ekonomik, sosyal ve politik faktörler etkilidir. Bu faktörler nedeniyle ortaya çıkan
göç, kentlerde çekme etkileri, kırda ise itme
etkileri ile açıklanabilir. Bu itici ve çekici faktörler
dikkate alınarak kişi bir yerden başka bir yere
hareket etmektedir. Nüfusu kente iten etkenler,
köyden kente artan nüfus baskısı, adil olmayan
toprak dağılımı, düşük verimlilik, doğal afetler,
kan davaları, toprağın mirasla parçalanması,
tarımda makineleşme sonucu işsizliğin artması ve
güvenliktir. Nüfusu kente çeken etkenler ise köy-
kent gelir farklılıkları, daha iyi eğitim, kentin ca-
zibesi, iş bulma ümidi, daha yüksek yaşam

standardı, ulaşım olanakları, kentlerdeki sosyal ve kültürel olanaklardan faydalanma isteğidir. Literatürde göç olgusu ele alan yaklaşımlardan biri fayda – maliyet yaklaşımıdır. Bu yaklaşıma göre bireylerin bulunduğu yerden başka bir yere göç kararı faydası maliyetinden yüksekse söz konusu olacaktır. Bu çalışmada, illerin sosyal, ekonomik ve fiziksel altyapı göstergeleri kullanılarak, 2008-2011 döneminde Türkiye'deki 81 ilin gelişmişlik göstergelerinin illerin aldığı ve verdiği göç üzerindeki etkisi count veri modelleri ile analiz edilmiştir.

***

Türkiye'deki Yabancıların Sosyal Güvenlik Hakları

(156) Müslim Demir (Celal Bayar University)

İlk ortaya çıktığı yıllarda daha çok işçi sorunları üzerinde duran sosyal politika kavramı zaman içerisinde toplumsal hayatı etkileyen her türlü sorunu kendisine konu edinmiştir. Bugün sosyal güvenlik, sosyal politikanın en etkin ve en kapsamlı bir aracıdır. Göç ise ülkelerin siyasal, sosyal, kültürel ve ekonomik yapılarıyla ilişkisi olan ve özellikle demografik yapılarına önemli etkileri olan bir kavramdır. Dolayısıyla göç kavramı sosyal politikanın en önemli aracı olan sosyal güvenlik politikasını da etkileyen bir kavramdır. Resmi kaynaklara göre son 13 yılda yaklaşık 2,5 milyon kişinin göç ettiği Türkiye'de sosyal güvenlik mevzuatı da buna bağlı olarak şekillenmiştir. Türkiye'deki sosyal güvenlik reformları ile yabancı uyruklu kişilerin çalışma şartlarına ve sosyal güvenlik haklarına ilişkin yeni düzenlemeler yapılmıştır. Bu çalışmada Türkiye'ye göç eden yabancı uyruklu kişilerin sosyal güvenlik hakları ele alınmış ve değerlendirmelerde bulunulmuştur.

***

Yeni Göç Hareketleri Perspektifinde Türkiye'deki Sığınmacılara Yönelik Kamusal Hizmetler

(154/9TP) Tülin Canbay (Celal Bayar University)

Göç insanlık tarihinin en eski sosyal olgularından biridir. Günümüzde de bu tarihsel hareketlilik güvenlik, insan hakları ve sosyo-politik faktörler gibi farklı nedenlerle de olsa geniş çapta devam etmektedir. Özellikle son dönemde Suriye'deki iç savaşın da etkisiyle göç eden sığınmacı sayısında önemli artışlar olmaktadır. Bu insanlar genellikle yakın ülkelere sığınmayı tercih etmişleridir. Bu ülkelerden biri de Türkiye'dir. Türkiye Suriyeli sığınmacıların en fazla göç ettiği ülkelerden biri olarak bir anda sayıları yüzbinlerle ifade edilen sığınmacıların barınma, beslenme, sağlık, ilaç temini, giyim ve eğitim gibi alanlarındaki ihtiyaçlarıyla karşı karşıya kalmıştır. Sığınmacıların eğitim farlılıkları, dil sorunları ve mevcut istihdam yasaları çerçevesinde iş gücü piyasasına yasal yollardan girebilmesi ya da iş bulabilmesi mümkün olmadığı için kendi imkanlarıyla bu ihtiyaçlarını giderebilmesi de mümkün olmamaktadır. Bu bağlamda sığınmacıların korunması ve bakımı devlet tarafından sunulan kamusal hizmetler kapsamında karşılanmak zorundadır. Ancak bu konuda uluslararası topluluk ve aktörlerin de bu kamusal hizmet yükünü paylaşma yönünde sorumluluklarının olduğu gözardı edilmemelidir. Bu çalışmada, özellikle Suriyeli sığınmacılar kapsamında Türkiye'deki göç hareketi analiz edilerek, devletin sunduğu hizmetler ve bu hizmetlerin maliyeti ele alınacaktır.

***

1989 Zorunlu Bulgaristan Göçünün Ekonomik ve Mali Yönünün İncelenmesine Yönelik Amprik Bir Araştırma

(12TP) Mustafa Miynat (Manisa Celal Bayar University) Öznur Akyol (Manisa Celal Bayar University), Deniz Alçın Şahintürk (Manisa Celal Bayar University)

İnsanlık tarihi kadar geçmişe dayanan göç olgusunun arka planında farklı tarih ve bu tarihin getirdiği farklı ekonomik ve sosyolojik nedenler yer almaktadır. Bu nedenlerle hemen hemen her coğrafyada yaşanan göç olgusu Türkiye için de her dönemde ciddi bir sorun teşkil etmektedir. Bulgaristan'dan Türkiye'ye gerçekleştirilen göç hareketleri de yaklaşık yüz elli yıl öncesine dayanmaktadır. İlk göç hareketi 1877-1878 Osmanlı-Rus savaşı sırasında gerçekleşmiştir. Cumhuriyet döneminde gerçekleşen, Suriye göçünden sonra ülkemize yönelik ikinci büyük göç hareketi 1950-51 yıllarında yaşanmıştır. Bunu takiben 1969-1978 yılları arasında da sayısı çok fazla olmasa da yakın akraba göçü olmuştur. Son dalga ise çalışmamızın da konusunu oluşturan 1989 zorunlu göç hareketidir. Bu göçün temelleri 1980'li yılların başında Jivkov yönetimindeki hükümet politikaları ile atılmıştır. Bulgaristan tarafından "Soya dönüş" adı altında uygulanan bu politikalar; Türklere yönelik doğrudan isim değiştirme yöntemi ile asimilasyon, isim değiştirmeyenlere maaşlarının ödenmemesi, bu nedenle işten çıkarmalar ve sağlık hizmetlerinden yararlanamama, fiziki zorlamaya dayalı sert uygulamalar, dinsel faaliyetlerin, Türklüğü temsil eden geleneksel kıyafetlerin ve Türkçe konuşmanın yasaklanması şeklinde gerçekleştirilmiştir.

Tüm bu baskılar sonucunda, Türk hükümetinin soydaşlara yönelik izlediği ılımlı politika, akrabalarının Türkiye'de bulunması ve Türkiye'deki eğitim ve iş imkânları soydaşlarımızın ülkemize göç etmelerine neden olmuştur. Türkiye'nin bu göç hareketine kayıtsız kalamaması beraberinde pek çok sosyo-ekonomik sonuçlar doğurmuştur. Çalışmada göç hareketinin Türkiye üzerindeki ekonomik ve mali etkileri ayrıntısı ile ele alınacaktır.
***

Why Grounded Theory Matters in Migration Studies? The Case of Migrant Women of Turkey and Domestic Violence

(101) Deniz Özalpman (University of Vienna)

This paper has two main strands: (1) to extend the practicality of the grounded theory methodology in migration studies and, (2) to contribute to the migrant women studies. Although grounded theory methodology became increasingly popular and is widely used in both qualitative and quantitative research paradigms with a growing interest, there is still scarcity of research focused on its application through migration studies. By referring more specifically to the third version of constructivist grounded theory (CGT), this article discusses related attributions for why domestic violence against women from Turkey with a migration background from the experts' perspective. In-depth interviews were conducted in the Austrian capital Vienna with experts from Wiener Interventionsstelle (Domestic Abuse Intervention Centre Vienna), Orient Express and Frauenhäuser Wien. Austria is one of the most developed countries in Europe to help migrant women on the issue of domestic violence with the capital Vienna receiving approximately 55% of the cases occurring in the country. In terms of methodology, CGT offers the best possibility to

make a holistic approach to the situation to the extent possible as the data is co-constructed with the researcher and participants/experts based on the interpretative understanding of the social phenomenon.
***

The Needs of LGBT Asylum Seekers in Turkey

(119) Sema Buz (Hacettepe University) and Nazlı Gizem Yıldırım (Hacettepe University)

LGBT -lesbian, gay, bisexual and transgender-individuals have different sexual orientation and mainstream society behave them discriminative ways related with heterosexist assumptions and gender stereotypes. These individuals escaped their countries of origin for fear of persecution and claim refugee status to destination countries. In refugee determination process sexual orientation and gender identity matters are determined "social causes" and they are not counted in vulnerable groups because of this they expose psychical and psychological violence in the whole process.

They have common difficulties with other asylum seekers and refugees in the asylum process but at the same time they have different experiences related to acceptance, lack of social support, exclusion from refugee community, accessibility to protection and social welfare services etc. The assumption about being refugee equal being political, devaluates diverse social groups and gender based refugee claims. However LGBTs experiences gender based violence in countries of origin and this violence accompanies their life cycle in different aspects.

In this paper the needs of LGBT asylum seekers are presented from findings of a qualitative research. This qualitative research implemented in Ankara and other satellite cities in central Anatolia. The needs of LGBT individuals will discuss gender and human rights frames in the paper.

***

Gendered Citizenship: Experiences and Perceptions of the Bulgarian Turkish Immigrant Women

(28) Özge Kaytan (Middle East Technical University)

The aim of this paper is to analyze the citizenship experiences and perceptions of the Bulgarian Turkish immigrant women with specific reference to their participation to the public sphere, their engagements in the private sphere, different socialization processes they have been through and their daily lives in Turkey. It is argued that the Bulgarian Turkish women's citizenship practices were constructed through their ethnic minority identity in Bulgaria, in Turkey their citizenship has become a gendered construct due to the gender norms imposed on immigrant women.

This study is based on feminist perspective and research procedure, challenging the conventional definitions of citizenship by including the experiences, thoughts, sensations, and the narratives of the immigrant women, and it is contended that the notion of citizenship should include such subjectivities. The fieldwork was conducted in the form of semi-structured interview surveys with 19 immigrants who immigrated to Izmir, Turkey from Bulgaria in 1989 and in the 1990s. The experiences of the immigrant women about their socio-economic conditions, identity perceptions, and their participation to the public spheres and the changing gendered dynamics in the private spheres constitute the core subjects for the analysis to demonstrate how they have experienced gendered citizenship in Turkey.

***

Corporeality and migration: psychosocial effects of social interventions in immigrant women

(131) Caterine Galaz Valderrama (University of Chile)

The installation process of the migrated population are framed in dynamic knowledge-power (Foucault, 1984), which ends up creating various possibilities of inclusion / exclusion. In this process is important the articulation of categories of differentiation such as gender, origin and class influences. In this junction of factors, the bodies of migrant women emerge as a focus of preferential attention and embody a process of greater social inequality that evidence derived framed in a subalternization and radical differentiation. Being considered socially as a "problem" to install the migrated people is managed from different frameworks for action: from security control policies to the policies and direct interventions professionalized.

In this matrix of power (Hacking, 1998) which includes among others laws and programs for professional care, the migrated people are controlled and disciplined in their forms of enunciation, visibility and performance, developing various devices accommodating these the majority group and liberal market logic. Not only the behaviors and bodies of people require adaptation and appear as objectified, but social interventions articulated with government and market logics, for the inclusion of this sector in peripheral spaces within the system are structured. Thus, the devices available for reception of people migrated, induce a certain ways of be, think and act as more acceptable than others, within the sociocultural context of installation.
***

SESSION 5A – Counter-Hegemonic Migrant Spaces, Place-Making and Resistance

Home-making as resistance

(98) Didem Kılıçkıran (Kadir Has University)

This paper examines the importance of the domestic home-space as a central site of resistance in the context of refugee migration. Revisiting the meanings of home in recent multi-disciplinary discussions on migration and mobility, together with the mainstream feminist understanding of home as a space women must be emancipated from in order to find their own identities, the paper looks at the ways in which Kurdish Alevi women in North London represent and renogiate their identities through home-making practices. Drawing on the results of an ethnographic fieldwork, the paper focuses particularly on the display of objects representing ethnic and religious identities and the use of diasporic forms of mediation as practices through which Kurdish Alevi women construct a resistance against both the suppression of their identities in homeland Turkey and the imperatives of the 'foreign' society outside. It also discusses practices of decoration and transformation of domestic spaces as indicators of these women's ongoing efforts to deal with the disparity between their own conceptions of a 'proper home' and the housing spaces available to them.

***

"The 'Rebellious Neighborhood' and Gentrification"

(4TP) Ülkü Güney (Abant Izzet Baysal University)

Neoliberal changes transform the participation on the society or shape new forms of democratic involvement. Since the beginning of the 1980s ideas based on neoliberalism became guiding principles for the urban social policy of local governments in Germany. Some areas considered as economically lucrative for the local government became battle grounds between stakeholders and the residents of the neighbourhood. The struggles of the residents against the appropriation of their neighbourhood through gentrification set off various kinds of new political projects in Hamburg's *Sternschanze* neighbourhood. The district is a densely populated neighbourhood with its high proportion on immigrants, under class Germans, students, drug users, anarchists and other culturally excluded and/or socially disadvantaged people. Simultaneously to the "house squatting struggles" a kind of cultural transformation found place enabled by the new economic chances. The district was "taken over" by a consumer-oriented alternative as well as by a political scene with the associated "ghetto feeling". These people were inspired by the idea to establish new models of emancipative, i.e., non-representative forms of political praxis. Later 'the scene' was fractured into various milieus such as political, hedonistic or aesthetic but remained loyal to the neighbourhood and open for other options (see Diederichsen, Subversions Reader, 1998). Immigrants and immigrants' organisations played a key role in shaping a counter hegemonic culture. The mere existence of these predominantly leftwing organizations was an indicator of the degree of political voice (Castaneda, 2012) in the neighbourhood. My paper is thus about the role of migrants' role in the overall struggle in the course of the neoliberal urban gentrification process. Moreover it is concerned with migrants' resistance practises, articulated, in various forms; culturally, socially and politically.

Gecekondus as Counter-Hegemonic Spaces and the Question of Resistance to Gecekondu Transformation Projects

(8TP) Tahire Erman (İhsan Doğramacı Bilkent University)

Gecekondus have been the counter-hegemonic spaces defined by the 'modern planned city' paradigm. As they were built by rural-to-urban migrants who lacked the 'urban cultural capital' and as they developed spontaneously on public land without any order, they were stigmatized as the place of the 'rural Other.' Today as cities are restructured under neoliberal imperatives, gecekondu neighborhoods are intervened by authorities to release the 'rent gap' and to remove those who are not 'appropriate' for the world city image of Turkish metropolises. The demolition of gecekondus is followed by gentrification. The question of resistance of residents has been on the agenda of academics and politicians since the mid-2000s when the first urban transformation project (Northern Ankara Entrance Urban Transformation Project) was introduced in the partnership of the National Housing Development Administration (TOKI) and the Greater Ankara Mayor in 2005. The factors that lead to resistance are identified in some (Kuyucu ve Ünsal, 2010) and the lack of it is explained in others (Karaman, 2014). The nature of this resistance, if any, is ambivalent. This paper makes its contribution by discussing the issue by emdedding it in ethnographic field studies that are conducted in three such sites that differ from each other in terms of the composition of residents (political views, religious/sectarian identity, hometown) as well as the compensations offered by or fought from authorities ("the politics of compensation") and the degree of organized resistance. The outcomes of gecekondu transformation, i.e., the counter-hegemonic spaces of migrants, are discussed in terms of the new positions of migrants and their new places in the city.

Demographic and human capital heterogeneity in selected provinces of Turkey: A scenario analysis using multi-dimensional population projection model

(32) M. Murat Yüceşahin (Ankara University) and Samir Kc (International Institute for Applied Systems Analysis)

Turkey is a geographically diverse country and two important components of that diversity is demographic and the level of education. Regions of the country vary markedly in the age structure of the population and even more conspicuously in such characteristics as fertility, mortality, and migration and the level of educational attainment. The purpose of this study is mainly to explore the effect of various demographic and education scenarios on the size and the structure of the population in five selected provinces (Ankara, Gaziantep, İzmir, Kayseri, and Van) that are representative of four fertility regions of Turkey. Three scenarios were defined namely: "Euro" in which Turkey joins European Union, "Medium" as a continuation of trend, and "3-Child"in which Turkey becomes more conservative. Based on our knowledge about the past and expectation in the future for each scenario, we defined set of assumptions for fertility, mortality, migration, and education and these assumptions were implemented in a multi-state population projection model to project the population by age, sex and educational attainment in five selected provinces from 2010 to 2050.

Under all scenarios, population in the five provinces will grow between 2010 and 2050. Under Euro and Medium scenario, the population of children will diminish and the population of elderly and those in the age-group 15-64 will increase in all scenarios. In terms of education, as expected a rapid transformation will take place under Euro scenarios with more homogenous and higher level of human capital across Turkey, whereas, under 3-Child scenario Turkey will continue to be a heterogeneous society with a lower level of human capital. The result of this exercise reveals the extent to which Turkey's population can evolve in the future and provides policy makers and planners with a tool to look into the future and test the implication of certain policies and expectations on the development of population.

***

Analyzing the contribution of migration to replacement of population in and across Turkey

(50) Dalkhat Ediev (Vienna Institute of Demography) and M. Murat Yüceşahin (Ankara University)

As in most other developing countries, the fertility rate in Turkey has seen dramatic declines over the past five decades. The fact that Turkey's total fertility rate declined from 6.28 to 2.08 children per woman between the early 1960s and the late 2000s shows that the country has experienced a rapid fertility transition. Thus, a number of studies note that Turkey is in the final phase of the demographic transition. Although Turkey has recently reached slightly below replacement level of fertility, there remain marked regional demographic differentials.

Beginning with the proclamation of the Turkish Republic in 1923, the inadequacy and imbalanced diffusion of social and economic developmental initiatives, meant to spread modernisation throughout the country, served to exacerbate the substantive regional inequalities to the detriment of the eastern regions. During this period, regional divergence in socio-economic development was accompanied by a marked inter-provincial migration and prominently concentrated migration flows, particularly from poor eastern provinces to the relatively developed western regions and particularly large metropolitan areas of the country. This process led to a rapid urbanisation process which resulted mainly from rural to urban migration and market adjustment to the inter-sector shift from agriculture to manufacturing and services. As a result, between 1950 and 2010, the percentage of urbanisation in the country increased from 25 to around 77. In the same period Turkey's population reached from 20.5 to around 76 million. In terms of the regional imbalances in the country, the most interesting change was the rise in the gap in fertility levels between the western and the south-eastern regions: fertility levels of very high fertility provinces were 1.73 times the levels in low fertility provinces in 1980, compared with 3.12 in 2000 (Yüceşahin and Özgür, 2008). This change clearly points to how the difference in demographic characteristics between Turkey's western and south-eastern regions has gradually widened over time.

In the study-subject field the relationship between migration and replacement of population has been attracting great attention scholarly. Thus, migration has become a key factor in the growth and replacement of populations. For example, some studies note that in most Western European countries, net migration greatly exceeds natural change, in some cases driving remarkable population growth or at least halting or slowing population decline. Migration can compensate for missing births in low-fertility areas, provinces or countries. Although past and recent general fertility trends, regional inequalities, and migration patterns in Turkey have been well documented in research through analysis of demographic sample surveys and censuses, the relationship between migration and the replace-

ment of population by region in the country has not been examined extensively. It is worthwhile to undertake the contribution of migration to population reproduction in Turkish context. Thereby, in this study, we aim to present a study of contribution of migration to replacement of population in and across Turkey. The regions (in NUTS 1 level) of Turkey are very much different in levels of fertility and migration that makes it very interesting to study the two processes in their geographic aspect. To this end, we use recently proposed methodology of studying the population replacement levels by the indicators of Combined Reproduction and Times to Half-Replacement (Ediev et al.,2014) that may be computed from a limited data and offer a good insights into demographic consequences of a given combination of fertility and migration levels.
***

Rural-to-Urban Migration in Turkey from 1965 to 2000

(152) Ayşe Gedik (Middle East Technical University)

This study analyzes rural-to-urban out-migration during thirty-five years between 1965-2000 in the five five-year periods of 1965-1970, 1975-1980, 1980-1985, 1985-1990, and 1995-2000. Rural-to-urban out-migration is studied in terms of village-to-province center out-migration. The data is from the Population Censuses which are 100% sample, and the migration data are based on the de jure population. Various measures such as the size and the distribution of the village population, out-migration rates, intra-province migration, and the significance of the three largest metropolises as destination points are analyzed.

The analyses are mainly descriptive accompanied with plausible hypotheses. The changes during the last thirty-five years, and consequently possible future trends are discussed.
***

SESSION 5C – Yeni Göç Eğilimleri

"Zorunluluk mu", "Gönüllü mü"? Türkiye'den BK'a Yeni Göç Dalgası: Ankara Anlaşması

(140) Tuncay Bilecen (Kocaeli University & Regent's University London)

1960'lı yıllarda Türkiyeli misafir işçiler açısından Almanya kadar cazip bir ülke olmayan İngiltere, 1970'li ve 1980'li yılların ardından başlayan politik göçlerin merkezlerinden birisi haline geldi. Özellikle Kürt bölgesindeki iç savaş ortamı 1990'lı yıllardan itibaren Kürt nüfusun yoğun olarak İngiltere'ye göçüne neden oldu.

Politik sığınmacı akınının durmasının ardından göç bir müddet aile birleşmeleri ve kaçak yollarla girişlerle devam etti. Göçü sınırlandırmaya yönelik politikaların hayata geçirilmesinin ardından Ankara Anlaşması'ndan yararlanarak İngiltere'ye göç etmek, oturum almanın en uygun yollarından biri haline geldi. Dolayısıyla; eğitim, dil öğrenmek, çocuk bakmak amacıyla gelenler İngiltere'de kalıcı olmak istediklerinde bu anlaşmadan yararlanma yoluna başvurdular.

Bu yeni göç dalgasıyla gelenlerin çoğunun eğitim düzeyi yüksek ve dil sorunu olmayan göçmenlerden oluştuğu görülmektedir. Göçmenler genellikle İngiltere'ye gelmek için akraba ya da hemşehricilik ilişkileri yerine daha çok kişisel niteliklerini (eğitim, meslek, kabiliyet vs.) kullanmaktadırlar. Öte yandan Türkiye'deki kariyerlerini bırakarak İngiltere'de yerleşmek niyetinde olan bu göçmenleri özellikle ilk birkaç yıl süresince önemli güçlüklerle karşılaşmaktadırlar.

Bu çalışmada, Ankara Anlaşması'ndan yararlanarak Londra'da oturum/ vatandaşlık alan veya almaya çalışan 20 göçmenle yapılan yarı yapılandırılmış mülakat (semi-stracturel interview) sonucunda elde edilen bugular ortaya konulacaktır.

Çalışmanın üzerinde odaklanacağı nokta; bu yeni göç dalgasının 'zorunlu' mu yoksa 'gönüllü' bir göç hareketi olduğudur. Bir başka deyişle çalışmada göçmenleri göç etmeye iten motivasyonlar (ekonomik, siyasal, sosyo-kültürel, psikolojik vs.) irdelenecektir. Göçmenlerin göçün ilk yıllarında Türkiyeli toplulukla kurduğu ilişkiler ise "ethnic enclave" bağlamında üzerinde odaklanılacak bir başka konu başlığıdır.

***

Eğitim İçin Türkiye'ye Gelen Uluslararası Üniversite Öğrencilerinin Uyum Düzeylerinin Değerlendirilmesi

(16TP) Emine Akman (Manisa Celal Bayar University)

Dünyanın farklı yerlerinden uluslararası öğrenciler Türkiye'ye daha iyi bir eğitim almak ve iş deneyimi kazanmak için gelmektedir. Bu süreçte yeni yer, eğitim koşulları, arkadaşlar değişik bir sistem gibi farklı sıkıntı ve problemler ortaya çıkmaktadır. Bu zorluklarla mücadele etmek oldukça stresli ve olumsuz psikolojik çıktıları olan bir süreç olarakta değerlendirilebilir. Bu süreçte yaşanan uyum problemlerinin ve düzeyinin ortaya konulması sürecin daha yumuşak şekilde geçebilmesinin sağlayacaktır.

Bu araştırma, Celal Bayar Üniversitesi'nde eğitim gören uluslararası öğrencilerin psikolojik uyum düzeylerini ortaya koyacaktır. Araştırmaya Celal Bayar Üniversitesi çeşitli fakültelerinde birinci sınıf öğrencisi olan 230 uluslararası öğrenci, (95 kadın, 135 erkek) katılmıştır. Araştırmanın istatistiksel analizlerinde tanımsal istatistiksel analiz yöntemleri ve bağımsız gruplar için t testi kullanılmıştır. Uluslararası öğrencilerin psikolojik iyi olma ve yaşam doyumu düzeylerinin farklılaştığı bulunmuştur.

***

Türkiye'ye Yönelik Uluslararası Emekli Göçü: Problem ve Fırsatlar

(14TP) Betül Dilara Şeker (Manisa Celal Bayar University), Halil İbrahim Bahar (Police Academy)

To take advantage of a better climate and enjoy the sunshine as one element of a healthier, happier lifestyle, it would seem that retired people what we call them "settled foreigners", from northern and western Europe are settling along Turkey's Aegean and Mediterranean coasts. This paper recounts the findings from a questionnaire administered to a random sample of 504 EU citizens who have settled full-time, or who spend a large part of each year, in Turkey. Researchers' personal observations and some extracts from interview data are also included. The work focuses on the demographics of the sample, their reasons for settling in Turkey, their perceived problems in adjusting to life in a foreign country, and looks at their relationships with their fellow countrymen and local Turkish communities. How are the settled foreigners treated by the Turkish community? The level of their satisfaction or dissatisfaction with the life in Turkey will be examined. This paper attempts to determine social, economic and political difficulties they confront and their problems concerning integration into the Turkish society.

Another aim of this study is to explore the way in which foreign settlers would participate into social, economic and political life in Turkey. Could settled foreigners be a bridge between Turkey and the European Union? What can be said about the role of settled foreigners in Turkey regarding Turkey's accession to the European Union?

***

Türkiye'de Ekonomik Kalkınmanın Bölgesel Göçlere Etkisi

(26TP) Hakan Aracı (Manisa Celal Bayar University), Coşkun Çılbant (Manisa Celal Bayar University), Uğur Bilgen (Manisa Celal Bayar University)

Göç, tüm dünyayı etkileyen gerek göç alan gerekse göç veren ülkeler açısından önemli bir olgudur. Söz konusu bu durum tüm toplumların, siyasi ve ekonomik karar mekanizmalarının merkezinde yer almaktadır. Siyasi iktidarın bu hususta verdiği veya vereceği kararlar göç edenleri ekonomik, sosyal ve kültürel açıdan olumlu veya olumsuz olarak direk etkileyecektir.

Göç olgusu genellikle ekonomik, sosyal ve siyasal nedenlerle ortaya çıkar. Ekonomik nedenler incelendiğinde temelinde, ülkeler arasındaki gelişmişlik farklılıklarından doğan sonuçlar yer almaktadır. İç göç olgusu da ülkeler arasında gerçekleşen göçte olduğu gibi, bölgeler arasındaki ekonomik kalkınma düzeyleri farklılıklarından kaynaklanmaktadır.

Ülkelerde bölgeler arası göçler genellikle sermayenin gelişmiş olduğu yerlere doğru hareketlenmektedir. İç göçün en büyük nedeni bölgelerin eşit olarak kalkınmayı sağlayamadıklarından kaynaklanmaktadır. İç göç az gelişmiş bölgeden yani emek yoğundan gelişmiş bölgelere doğru yani sermaye yoğun bölgelere doğru olacaktır.

Çalışmada Türkiye'nin bölgeler arasında yaşanan göçlerin ekonomik etkileri üzerinde durulmuştur. Bu ekonomik etki; bölgelerin sanayi, turizm, hizmet gibi sektörlerdeki gelişmişlik farkları esas alınarak yapılmış ve inceleme konumuzu oluşturmuştur. Bu özelliklere sahip yani sanayi, turizm ve hizmet sektörünün geliştiği bölgeler incelenirken, o bölgelere yapılan göçler ile aynı zamanda göçe maruz kalan kesimlerin mevcut bölgeleri incelenmiştir. Bölgeler arasındaki bu ekonomik farklılıkların, göçler üzerindeki etkisi incelenmiştir.

***

The Event of Bulgaria Migration and the Discourses of Nationalism and Gender in Ahmet Er's Theater Script

(49) Başak Akar (Yıldırım Beyazıt University), Özge Öz Döm (Yıldırım Beyazıt University) and Melike Güngör (Yıldırım Beyazıt University)

Putting migration at the center of this study, where the changing political situation forces masses to migrate from Bulgaria to Turkey during1923-1952, we will investigate how Ahmet Er's theater play script utters migration, discourses of nationalism and gender by adopting narrative analysis. The aim of the study is to discern the relationship between nationalism and gender discourse in the migration phenomenon, where the historical outlook from the eye of the writer would be the base of the fiction.

We choose a theater script in order to make an evaluation, since Ahmet Er's script of "The Immigrant" have (re)presentative imagination, a probable affect on the audience by either watching or reading the play where the characters and the space fiction is more direct within dialogues as well as the preface and the details amongst the dialogues.
***

Tracing Deep Scars of 1915 in Art and Literature

(103) Esin Gülsen (Middle East Technical University), Erdem Çolak (Ankara University) and Selen Yamak

Regardless of whether we call it genocide, massacre, exile or deportation, events experienced in Ottoman lands in 1915 cost countless lives, forced millions of Armenian people to leave their lands and left deep marks on next generations. Art and literature are great tools both to exhibit traces of exile and deportation and to come to terms with scars of these events for people who continue to live on the lands forcibly left behind by exiles. There are two critical roles of art and literature. First of all, collective memory shared by communities which lived together in the past may be preserved with the help of art and literature. Secondly, they have a critical curative role for deep psychological scars of exiles so they are irrevocable both for individual and collective healing.

In this study, we will trace marks of Armenian genocide and deportation mainly through works of art of two world-known Armenian artists. Archile Gorky, a world-famous painter, was just seven years old when he was forced to leave city of Van in Turkey with his mother in 1915 and lost her mother after a short time. His paintings reflect the deep trauma of the genocide and loss

of his mother. William Saroyan whose family had gone to the US before 1915 projects signs of genocide in his novels and stories. Deep psychological scars of the genocide, exile and homesickness are very clear in works of these two Armenian artists. In the 100th anniversary of the sad events of 1915, it is critical to turn our face to works of Armenian artists both to cure our scars and come to terms with the past. It is our responsibility to remember, remind and preserve art and culture of people who were forced to leave their lands on which we still live.
***

Representations of "Welat" (Homeland) in Kurdish Classical and Modern Poetry

(107) Farangis Ghaderi (Soran University/ University of Exeter)

Homeland (welat/weten) from its classical designation as one's birthplace in the Kurdish Kurdish poetry moved toward its modern definition as a bounded geographical territory in the poetry of the late nineteenth and early twentieth century. It was developed to a gendered entity in modern poetry and was imagined as a female body; as a mother, often ill and in need of care, or a woman beloved whose honour "namus" was the subject of male protection. The new definition of "Welat/weten" (homeland) played an important role in developing Kurdish nationalism as it provided the nationalists with a powerful tool to urge Kurdish people to fight for their homeland and to protect it against intruders. This paper is an in-depth study of the development of the concept of "welat" from its pre-modern meaning to a modern homeland in Kurdish classical and modern poetry. The process of this transformation and its context, and its contribution to the Kurdish nationalistic discourse will be studied in the works of the prominent modern Kurdish poets. The study is focused on Kurdish poetry because poetry was the predominant literary genre of Kurdish literature before the twentieth century

SESSION 6A – Migration and Religious Identity

Turkish Mosques in Britain as a Religious Socialization Agent

(80) Yakup Çoştu (Hitit University) and Elif Büşra Kocalan (Hitit University)

Mosque, as a religious place, is one of the constituent institutions of the social structure of Muslim society. It is not only a place where in religious practices are carried out by participants, but it also has a significant role in formation of their Islamic identity, and in creation and preservation of the sacred memory of the community.

It is known that Turkish Muslim immigrants living in various European countries have established mosques/religious places. These places have some different social functions besides being houses of worship. In this regard, religious institutions represent a space where culture and values from the homeland are shared, where courses and educational activities are carried out, possible problems that are experienced in the host countries can be solved and religious and cultural differences towards host countries are symbolized

In this paper, it will be focused on the mosques which are established by Turkish Muslim immigrants in Britain as a religious socialization agent. In this context, the paper will try to search for answers to the following questions: What kind of Islamic discourse Turkish mosques in Britain have? Are there any differences among religious, social and cultural activities carried out by mosques/mosque unions according to their owned religious discourse? How are the impact of these mosques, as a religious socialization factor, on the Turkish Muslim immigrants' religious orientation and religious identity? This research is methodologically based on empirical evidence. In the answering abovementioned questions, observations, which were obtained from field researches on-going for a long time about this issue, will be used.
***

Conflicts over Mosque Constructions by Turkish-Muslim organizations in Austria

(134) Ernst Fürlinger (Danube University Krems)

Like in other European countries, there are intense conflicts over the institutionalization of Islam in the form of physical buildings, beginning in 2005 with the construction of the first minaret in Tyrol by former labour migrants from Turkey. These processes can be understood as public negotiations about the question of belonging to the ‚national community‘, where borders and certain imaginations of this ‚community‘ are re-affirmed or changed. The paper presents an overview of the development of this field of conflict in Austria, distinguishing several phases of the conflict dynamics at different places which are part of a whole, slowly developing conflict system. In a second step, the paper describes a multi-dimensional framework for the analysis of mosque construction conflicts in European migration societies, combining variables at the macro-level (e.g. the activity of transnational networks of global djihadist organizations, the „war on terror“ and its local effects; ideological and political developments of the AKP in Turkey and its perception in Austrian local politics), meso-level (e.g. the specific migration regime in the 1950s and 1960s in Austria and its aftermath; the specific phantasm and imagination of the ‚Turks‘/Ottomans in the collective national

memory in Austria and its political instrumentalisation) and micro-level (e.g. the specific players and political power relations at the local level).
***

Migration, Identity and Islam in Europe

(96) Esma Durugönül (Akdeniz University)

Identity is one of the most important concepts in social sciences especially since the 1980s. Particularly in the context of migration in the globalized world and transnationalism being one of the most characteristic features of migration today, identity has turned out to be one of the most complex topics. Following the attack on the offices of Charlie Hebdo, and the following incidents in Paris/France, it has become urgent more than ever to rethink and reconsider the phenomenon of identity in Europe concerning immigrants from an Islamic background. The main aim of this paper is to contribute to the understanding of the roots and reasons of religious radicalism among migrants in Europe. Therefore, this paper investigates the issue of identity formation, identity reconstruction and other questions concerning identity in the migration process against the background of traumatic historical events and contemporary political events in the world that have an impact on the Muslims perception of the West and particularly of Europe. This paper will shed light on Europeans' perception of Islam and Muslims as well as migration policies which lead to marginalising migrants in Europe and further to critically evaluate remedies and measures that have been adopted in order to secure especially the migrant youth in Europe from becoming radicalized.

***

Transnational Islamic Movements

(1) İnci Aksu Kargın (Indiana University Bloomington)

Even though the term "transnationalism" was originally linked to immigration, today the concept generally refers to the multiple ties and interactions that connect people or institutions across the borders of modern nation-states (Yilmaz, 2010). When one talks about transnationalism, Islam is one of the few words that come to mind. Like transnationalism itself, transnational Islam refers to the numerous dimensions it takes. Bowen focuses on three of these dimensions: demographic movements, transnational religious institutions, and Islamic reference and debate (2004). According to the first dimension of transnational Islam, Muslims move across borders for social and economic reasons and not reasons directly associated with Islam. The second dimension states that some Muslims who belong to religious organizations promote cross-national movements as part of their religious practices. The third dimension is the creation of an imagined Islamic community, known as the "umma," among ordinary Muslims who share the same duties and practices of Islam without necessarily migrating or forming Islamic movements.

In this paper, I will stress the second dimension of transnational Islam by analyzing the three main transnational Islamic movements: the Gulen Movement, Hizb-ut Tahrir and Tablighi Jamaat. First, I will discuss each movement by providing general information about the ideologies behind the movement as well as the structure and transnational activities of the movement. Then, I will analyze the movement in regard to its politics, violence and attitude toward women.

According to my research, even though these three transnational Islamic movements have similarities, many differences also exist between their ultimate objectives and the types of ventures that they embarked upon in order to achieve their goals. When summarizing the movements, all three movements have a hierarchical structure, voluntary membership and local groups. Moreover, While the Gulen Movement claims that it does not have an aim to establish a worldwide Islamic state and implement Sharia, both the Hizb ut Tahrir and Tablighi Jamaat movements mean to found an Islamic state by restoring the Caliphate. In addition, while the Gulen Movement is never mentioned in regard to violence,

the activities of the Hizb ut Tahrir and Tablighi Jamaat movements have been linked to terrorism, even though they were not originally founded as terrorist organizations. Moreover, even though, in all three movements, participation by women is allowed, a common mentality exists that the main role of women should be to take care of their children rather than seeking high positions within the movement. Finally, even though all of these movements represent themselves as apolitical, they always keep abreast of political changes by forming political parties in some countries (such as Hizb ut Tahrir), supporting specific Islamic political parties (such as the Gulen Movement), or having members from politics to influence the political decisions (such as Tablighi Jamaat).
***

A Transnational Actor: Monsieur Imam

(102) Irmak Evren (Middle East Technical University)

The ideal that determines the French model of nation, elaborated in "One and indivisible Republic" and "laicité"; with the emergence of "segmented society" fostered by the immigrants, now sheds light on the transformation which gives possibility for the co-existence of "unity" and "differentiation" in France. This transformation, substantially is prone to immigration patterns, would stress on the recognition of identities and in the context of Muslim migrants in France, puts religion to the forefront. Concurrently, identity politics concerning Turkish migrants started to cyristallize on account of the legislation in 1961 in Turkey, permitting the movement of Turkish citizens to Western Europe as "guest workers" Such a movement as Dubet (1989a:59) puts forward, induces immigrants to be torn between two cultural and social worlds where they want to be a part of the new world without losing their identities. Herein, as religious identities are considered; endeavours of the first generation of Turkish Muslim migrants in search of places to perform their religious duties in the factories they work to the creation of "salle de prière" in the foyers they live, continually leads to the establishment of "cultural" "friendship" and "solidarity" associations in which the mosque, Turkish market and "lokal"s become the integral part. Initially, supported by the National Vision (Milli Görüş Hareketi) movement in France, yet its entailment to ideological differences, paves the way for the recreated transnational organization- DITIB France (Turkish Islamic Union for Religious Affairs); an umbrella organization of 150 associations, including "Amicale de Franco-Turque" located in Carrières-sous-Poissy, Paris. In this article, a study based on oral history which would aim to contribute to the dialogue of empirical and theoretical framework to further illustrate the significance and functioning of a transnational organization by focusing on a transnational actor; a "religious official" assigned by the Presidency of Religious Affairs in Turkey to conduct religious service to Turkish-Muslim migrants in Paris for four years, between 2007-2011.

***

SESSION 6B – Kamu Hizmetleri ve Göç

Van İlinde Yaşayan İranli Şartli Mültecilerin Sosyo-Demografik Özellikleri Bakimindan Kamu Hizmetlerinden Memnuniyet Ve Uyumlarinin İstatistiksel Analizi

(100) Rıdvan Keskin (Manisa Celal Bayar University) and Güven Şeker (Manisa Celal Bayar University)

Türkiye uluslararası alanda göç süreçleri ve bu süreçlerden etkilenen ülkelerden biri olarak 2013 yılında Cumhuriyetin kuruluşundan bu tarihe kadar kanun düzenlemeleri olmadan ikincil düzenlemeler ile göç alanını düzenlemekteydi. Özellikle bu alanda uluslararası yükümlülüklerini yerine getiren Türkiye alandaki uyum, bütünleşme, sosyal ve ekonomik ihtiyaçlar, farklı grupların beklentilerinin yerine getirilmesi gibi medeni, ekonomik, sosyal hakların yanında temel insan haklarına uygun olan/olabilecek gereklilikleri ne yazık ki yerine getirmekten uzak kaldığı

farklı çalışmalarda da belirtilmektedir. Çalışma özellikle Türkiye bütününü yansıttığı önceki çalışmalarda da ifade edilen Van ili ve belirtilen ilde ikamet eden İran'dan ülkeye sığınan şartlı mültecilere sunulan kamusal hizmetler ve bu hizmetler ile ilgili farklı demografik özelliklere göre memnuniyet ve uyumlarını istatistiksel olarak ele almıştır. Yapılan istatistiksel analizlerle ankete katılan göçmenlerin demografik özelliklerine göre anket sorularına verdikleri cevaplar arasında anlamlı fark olup olmadığı ki-kare test istatistiği ile araştırılmıştır. Ki-kare test istatistiği ile 84 hipotez kurularak test edilmiştir. Bu test sonucunda da 20 hipotezde anlamlı farklılık olduğu belirlenerek, bu farklılıklar açıklanmıştır.
***

Türkiye'de Belediyelerin Yabancılara Yönelik Hizmet Sunumu: Sorunlar ve Çözüm Önerileri

(15TP) Güven Şeker (Manisa Celal Bayar University), Mustafa Ökmen (Manisa Celal Bayar University)

Yerel yönetim birimi olan Belediyeler hizmet sunmak için görev yapan yerel yönetim birimleridir. Belediyelerin sundukları hizmetler ulusal mevzuatların gereği olduğu kadar küresel hale gelen dünyada herkes tarafından beklen(ebilecek)en faaliyetlerdir.

İnsanlar yerleşik yaşadıkları kadar bu gün artık hareketli bir halde farklı yerlerde hayatlarını devam ettirebilmektedirler. İnsanlar yeni geldikleri yere emek, sermaye ve birikim getirmektedirler, bu değerlerin geldiği yerde de yaşamlarını menşe yerlerinde sürdürdüklerine benzer istendik şekilde geçirebilmek için hizmet beklerler. Türkiye küreselleşme, sermayenin ülkeye çekilmesi, uluslararası alanda yapılan sözleşme ve antlaşmaların gereği gibi etkenler ile ulusal mevzuatta farklı düzenlemeleri de gerektiğinde yaparak yerel yönetimlerde hareketli gruplara göre düzenleme yapabilmektedir.

Çalışma karşılaştırmalı olarak yerel yönetimlerin yükümlü oldukları hizmetleri yerine getirirken yerel halk dışında kalan yabancı gruplara hizmet sunumunda yaklaşımları, bu yaklaşımlardaki değişimleri ele alarak geleceğe yönelik bakış açıları ile ele alacaktır.
***

Küresel Kamusal Açmaz: Suriyeli Mülteciler Ve Türkiye

(136) Sibel Aybarç Bursalıoğlu (Celal Bayar University)

2010 yılı sonunda Tunus'ta iktidar karşıtı gösterilerle başlayıp Libya, Mısır, Suriye'nin de içinde bulunduğu geniş coğrafyayı etkisi altına alarak liderlerin devrilmesine yol açan Arap Baharı, küresel ölçekte sosyal, siyasi, kültürel, askeri ve ekonomik boyutta ciddi etkiler meydana getirmiştir. Bu kaotik süreç, yakın coğrafyada bulunan Türkiye'yi askeri tedbirler, petrol ithalatı ve en önemlisi Arap Baharı'nın yaşandığı ülkelerden gelen mülteciler konusunda zor durumda bırakmıştır. Ancak Türkiye, insani yardım kapsamında olayların başladığı ilk günden itibaren iç savaştan etkilenen Suriyeliler için "açık kapı" politikası izlemiştir. Suriye'den Türkiye'ye göç edenlerin sayısı (yasadışı gelenler de dahil) 1.200.000'i aştığı tahmin edilmektedir. Bu mültecilerden yalnızca 804.391'i kayıtlı olup, kayıtlı Suriyeli mültecilerin 221.442'si Nisan 2014 tarihi itibariyle 10 ilde 22 barınma merkezinde hayatına devam etmektedir. Birleşmiş Milletler verilerine göre Türkiye, 2011 yılından günümüze kadar Başbakanlık Afet ve Acil Durum Yönetimi Başkanlığı (AFAD) üzerinden Suriyeli mülteciler için barınma, sağlık, eğitim başta olmak üzere 3 milyar doları aşan tutarda harcama yapmıştır. Türkiye ekonomisi söz konusu sosyal yardımların yanı sıra, mültecilerin ucuz işgücü arzı dolayısıyla, kayıt dışı istihdam artışından da olumsuz etkilenmektedir. Bu durum, bir taraftan işsizlik oranını yükseltirken, diğer taraftan vergi gelirlerinin düşmesine neden olmaktadır. Türkiye'de bulunan Suriyeli mülteciler için Birleşmiş Milletler ve uluslararası yardım kuruluşlarının katkı sağlama konusunda yetersiz kalması, Türkiye'nin kamusal gelir ve gider dengelerini olumsuz etkilemekte ve yükünü arttırmaktadır. Çalışma kapsamında, Suriye iç savaşından kaçıp, Türkiye'ye sığınan mültecilerin Türk ekonomisi özellikle kamu maliyesi dengeleri açısından meydana getirdiği etkiler incelenmektedir.

***

SESSION 6C – Türkiye'de Göç ve İşgücü Piyasaları

Yabancı Ülkelerden Türkiye'ye Göç Eden Kişilerin Çalışma ve Sigortalılık Durumları

(2TP) Füsun Gökalp (Manisa Celal Bayar University)

Türkiye son yıllarda hem bölgesinde cazibe merkezi olmaya başlaması hem de komşu ülkelerin iç sorunları nedeniyle yüksek miktarda göç almaya başlamıştır. Gelen göçlerin % 44.1'i büyük şehirlere, % 33.4'ü il ve ilçe merkezlerine gerçekleşmektedir. En fazla göç alan illerimiz sırasıyla İstanbul, Bursa ve İzmir olmuştur. Özellikle bu şehirlerin göç almasının nedeni iş olanaklarının daha yüksek olmasıdır. Göç eden kişiler ülkemizde çalışmak için çalışma izni almak zorundadır. Çalışma izni verilen toplam yabancı sayısı 2004 yılında 7.302 iken, on yıl sonra 45.834 olmuştur. Bu rakamlar bize yurt dışından Türkiye'de çalışmak için göç edenlerin sayısının her geçen gün arttığını göstermektedir.

Ülkemizde yabancıların çalışmaları 4817 sayılı Yabancıların Çalışma İzinleri Hakkında ki Kanun ile takip edilmektedir. Bu kanun ile yabancılara çalışma izinlerinin Çalışma ve Sosyal Güvenlik Bakanlığı tarafından verilmesi ve yabancı çalışma izinleri ile ilgili tek bir kurumun yetkili olması sağlanmıştır. Diğer kurumların çalışan yabancılar ile ilgili bilgileri Çalışma ve Sosyal Güvenlik Bakanlığı ile paylaşma zorunluluğu getirilmiş ve kontrol tek bir yapıda toplanmıştır. Dolayısıyla ülkemizde yabancı çalıştırmak isteyen işverenlerin bu konuya dikkat etmeleri gerekmektedir. Ancak ülkemize göç edip çalışma izni almadan ve sigortalı olarak çalıştırılmayan diğer bir ifade ile kaçak çalıştırılan insanlar mevcuttur. Çalışma izni olmaksızın, yabancı işçi çalıştıran işverenlere para cezaları uygulanmaktadır. Bu konuda ülkemizde yabancı işçi çalıştırmak isteyen işverenlere yardımcı olmak amaçlanmıştır. Bu itibarla yabancı çalışanların çalıştırılması halinde uyulacak prensip ve kurallar bu çalışmanın konusunu oluşturmaktadır.

Londra'da Çalışan Türkiyeli Göçmenlerin Çalışma Süreleri ve Sosyal İlişkileri

(1TP) Mehmet Rauf Kesici (Kocaeli University & Regent's University London)

Göçmenlerin emek piyasalarındaki konumları, çalışma koşulları ve çalışma süreleri ekonomik ve sosyal açıdan çeşitli sonuçlar doğurmaktadır. Bu çerçevede Londra'da yaşayan Türkiyeli göçmenlerin çalışma süreleri ele alındığında kitlenin bazı genel göçmen özelliklerinin yanı sıra kendine özgü bazı özellikler taşıdığı görülmektedir. Bu genel ve lokal özelliklerin birleşiminin göçmenlerin ekonomik ve sosyal yaşantılarında nasıl sonuçlar yarattığı ve bu özelliklerin sosyal ilişkilere nasıl yansıdığı, nasıl yaşandığı önem arz etmektedir.

Bu çalışma, Londra'da sürdürülen bir alan araştırmasından elde edilen bulguların derlenmesiyle oluşturulacaktır[2]. Bu çerçevede Londra'da çalışan Türkiyeli göçmenlerin çalışma sürelerinin ve günlerinin, bu göçmen topluluğun sosyal ilişkilerinde nasıl sonuçlar yarattığını irdelemek araştırmanın temel sorusunu oluşturmaktadır. Göç literatürü sosyal ve ekonomik değişmelerle yenilenen, farklılaşan dinamik bir alandır ve çalışmanın gerekçesi biçiminde, bu çalışmayla, ilgili alana güncel bir katkı yapılması hedeflenmektedir. Devam eden alan çalışmasından elde edilen ilk bulgular, ilgili göçmenler arasında çalışma süreleri ve günlerinin günlük yaşamın önemli belirleyicilerinden biri olduğunu ve hayatın birçok alanına çeşitli etkiler yaptığını göstermektedir.

---

[2] Bu alan araştırması, "Londra'da Yaşayan Türkiyeli Göçmenlerin Emek Piyasalarındaki Konumlarının Belirleyicileri" başlıklı, Regent's University London, Regent's Centre for Transnational Studies'da yürütülen, TÜBİTAK, 2219-Yurt Dışı Doktora Sonrası Burs Programı tarafından desteklenen bir araştırma projesidir.

Beş Sınır Kenti ve İşgücü Piyasalarında Değişim: 2011-2014

(71) Kuvvet Lordoğlu (Kocaeli University)

Bu çalışma, resmi işgücü verilerinin bir bölümünün beş sınır kenti üzerinden değerlendirilmesi ile oluşturulmuştur. Burada amaçladığımız, özellikle Suriye iç savaşının iş piyasaları üzerindeki etkilerini görmek ve değerlendirmektir. Bu bağlamda incelenen beş sınır kenti, en çok Suriyeli göçmenin bulunduğu veya yerleştirildiği kentlerdir. Bu kentler Suriyeli Göçmen sayıları itibarı ile en çok nüfusu barındıran Gaziantep, Hatay, Şanlıurfa, Mardin ve Kilis illeridir. (AFAD Türkiye'deki Suriyeli Sığınmacılar 2013 Araştırma Raporu) Bu illere ait işgücü verileri 2011 ve 2014 yılları arasında değerlendirilecek ve değişimin sonuçları tartışmaya açılacaktır.

Bilindiği gibi Çalışma ve Sosyal Güvenlik Bakanlığı yayınladığı genelge ile, ikamet izni alan Suriye vatandaşlarının ikametleri sürelerince kısıtlayıcı bir değerlendirme olmadan çalışma izni alabilecekleri anlaşılmaktadır. Özellikle Güney Doğu Anadolu bölgesinde diğer bölgelere göre daha yüksek işsizlik oranları düşünüldüğünde Suriyeli göçmenlerin iş piyasalarına dahil olmaları, mevcut yapıyı daha kırılgan hale getirecek ve bölge illerinde iş arayanlarla göçmenler arasında çatışmalara zemin hazırlama ihtimalini arttıracaktır. Özellikle mevcut olan ücret ve çalışma koşullarının olumsuzluğunun enformel bir ekonomi içinde daha da yükselmesi beklenebilir.

Bu bildirinin, mevcut durum üzerinden iş piyasası koşullarının düzenlenmesine zemin hazırlayıcı bir arayış metni olması düşünülmektedir.

***

Türkiye'nin Göç Gerçeği ve İşgücü Piyasaları Açısından Değerlendirilmesi

(153) Gülşen Gerşil (Manisa Celal Bayar University)

Türkiye 1950'li yıllarla birlikte modern anlamda iç göç dönemine girmiş ve ülkenin yerleşim yapısı ve nüfus hareketleri bu dönemden sonra hızlı nüfus artışı ve tarım kesiminde yaşanan olumsuz dönüşümler nedeniyle önemli bir değişime uğramıştır.

Göçler, kırdan kente göç eden erkek nüfus üzerinde bir işçileşme sonucu meydana getirirken, ailenin diğer bireylerini de çalışma yaşamına sürüklemektedir. Göçler, yüksek oranlı işsizlik, artan yoksullaşma, gelir dağılımı adaletsizliği ve eğitim masrafları çocuk işgücünün yaygınlaşmasına neden olmaktadır. Çocuk işçiliği özellikle eve iş verme uygulamalarında ve kayıtdışı sektörde yaygın bir şekilde görülmektedir.

Türkiye'nin içinde bulunduğu coğrafya nedeniyle özellikle küreselleşme süreciyle birlikte ve Arap baharı, Sovyetler Birliği'nin dağılması vb.

sosyo-politik ve ekonomik nedenlerle oldukça fazla dış göç aldığı bilinmektedir. Ayrıca Türkiye'nin Avrupa Birliği ülkelerine gitmek isteyen göçmenlerin düzensiz olarak geçici ve transit geçiş yolu olarak kullandıkları bir ülke durumuna düştüğü görülmektedir.

1960-90 yılları arasında diğer ülkelere önemli ölçüde işgücü olarak kaynaklık eden Türkiye 1990 sonrasında komşularındaki siyasal ve ekonomik değişmelerin de etkisi ile gelen göçmenlerin bir bölümü işgücü piyasalarını dengesini bozacak biçimde çalışma hayatına dahil olmuşlardır. Düzensiz göçmenlerin özellikle nitelik gerekmeyen işler başta olmak üzere hizmet sektörüne enformel (kayıt dışı) olarak girmeleri kısaca görünür olmaları bir süre kamusal alanda işgücü piyasalarının işleyişi açısından birtakım sorunları da beraberinde getirmiştir. Özellikle 2011 yılından itibaren Iraklı ve Suriyeli sığınmacı göçmenlerin büyük rakamlara ulaşması, olayın sosyal ve ekonomik boyutlarını arttırdığı gibi insanlık dramları da oldukça düşündürücüdür.

Bütün bu tespitlerin ışığında, göçmenlik olgusu ile ortaya çıkan sorunların işgücü piyasalarına yansıması ele alınacaktır. Göçmenlerin işgücü piyasalarına uyumunu sağlayacak tedbirlerin, başta kayıt dışı istihdamlarının önlenmesi olmak üzere, çalışma izinleri ve sosyal güvenlik kapsamına alınmaları vb. acil düzenlemeler ve politikaların neler olabileceği konusu tartışılacaktır.

***

Identity and Community Building through Political Commitment. Case of Kurdish Migrants from Turkey in Marseille, France

(74) Zuhal Karagöz (Aix-Marseille Universite)

Based on a long term field work (April 2011-September 2014) among Kurdish migrants from Turkey settled in Marseille, this presentation will expose the multiplicity of community and identity building processes. For this purpose, it will focus on the political commitment in the Diaspora context and within a transnational space of mobilizations related to the ongoing Kurdish-Turkish conflict. This communication proposes to combine micro (migrants), meso (networks) and macro (national frames) levels of analysis for a better understanding of these processes including both individual and collective strategies.

This paper will assume the existence of a latent community based on political commitment that is a structuring component of the Diaspora as it is perceived in our study. Based on this assertion, the strong moments and the flat periods of the community building process will be questioned. The presentation will expose the combination of traditional practices as protesting mobilizations with emerging forms like politically connoted cultural practices. It will also consider the micro and/or ephemeral practices derived from affective/emotional register. Analyzing these multiple dynamics draws attention on the permanent and strategic renegotiations of the community and the common by its own members.

In what way(s) the Kurdish association as the node of political networks tries to strengthen the community allegiances by building an empowering discourse? How the political commitment becomes a tool for distinction within the Kurdish community and with the other migrant communities in Marseille - a city built on several migration flows? Does the political commitment act also as a sociation instrument? How does promoting the Kurdish cultural practices allow an opening-up from traditional forms of political mobilizations?
***

Transnational spaces between Dersim and Vienna

(37) Maria Six-Hohenbalken (Institute for Social Anthropology)

The migration of Kurds to Austria is marked, to a great extent, by bilateral working contracts between Turkey and Austria since the late 1960's as well as official refugee movements from Iraq, Iran and Syria. Concerning demographic issues it is estimated that at least 60.000 persons of Kurdish decent are now living in Austria. Kurds from Turkey did not easily gain refugee status in Austria, the figures of recognised refugees are much lower as in Germany e.g., so most of them who came to Austria officially tried to secure a living within the framework of bilateral contracts or through chain migration. Various diasporic associations and networks developed. Mainly in the last decade Kurdish communities from Dersim elaborated various educational, cultural and environmental projects. Beside initiatives for the language maintaining and development of Zaza and for the Alevi heritage (language courses, radio station, online TV, publications) also various environmental initiatives and small-scale village renewal projects in Dersim are organized in Vienna. These initiatives are closely connected to a political discourse in elaborating the fateful history in Dersim 1937/38.

Due to the long silencing and denial of the genocidal processes it is up to the next generations to elaborate on Dersim's history. Members of the first generation have already retired and remigrated or are oscillating between their homes in Dersim and in Vienna. Community development projects realized by the following generation(s) mirror the dealing with the fate of their ancestors, with untold family histories and orally transmitted knowledge of the persecution.

This presentation is based on fieldwork with Kurdish communities in Vienna focusing on these Austrian initiatives, their transnational entanglements as well as discursive spaces in order to elaborate specific 'Dersim' identities, shaped by Alevism, the Zaza language and the fateful history.

***

Kurdish Community in the Czech Republic and its Transnational Practice

(57) Michael Murad (Masaryk University)

Paper deals with Kurdish community residing in the Czech Republic – especially focuses on the promotion of their political interests. Paper is based on my long-term own field research. Used were mainly semi-structured interviews and analysis of documents. Attended were also various events organised by Kurds. The main task of case study is a description and analysis of the genesis of the Kurdish diaspora in the CR together with the analysis of the promotion of their political interests and their transnational activities of this relatively small not traditional Central European community. They seeks to promote organized interests, they are linked to the wider Kurdish diaspora in other countries and furthermore they are linked to their home countries as well, and therefore we are able to identify their transnational political, socio-cultural and economic activity. Kurdish community in the Czech Republic has established itself as a result of both voluntary and forced emigration mainly from Turkey, Syria, Iraq and Iran. The first Kurdish students who were politically active came to former Czechoslovakia in the 60s of the 20th century. In Czechoslovakia there also lived various prominent Kurdish politicians or artists and there were many visits of Kurdish politicians straight from Kurdistan also. This was enabled by attitude of the Czechoslovak communist government that was supportive toward Kurdish claims in the Middle East. After the revolutionary events of 1989, the Kurdish community composition changed – more Kurds from Turkey arrived. Members of the Union of Kurdish Students established in the 2003 Kurdish civil association, which represents the only functioning organization. Contrary to the situation in the Western Europe, Kurdish civil association is composed of Kurds from Turkey, Iraq, Syria and Iran together, what brings some difficulties. Since 2011 are Kurds residing in the Czech Republic also very active in protests against regime of Bashar al-Assad.

***

The well-being of young Kurdish and Turkish migrant men in Europe

(77) Necla Açık (University of Manchester), Jonathan Spencer (University of Manchester), Jo Deakin (University of Manchester) and Claire Fox (University of Manchester)

In public debates, young migrant men (YMM) frequently feature as a problematic group, failing in the education system, potentially upholding sexist attitudes, and exhibiting violent and criminal behaviour. Research has pointed out that the experiences of YMM are influenced by negative stereotyping and they face discrimination significantly more often than their female counterparts. At the same time, YMM have to cope with high expectations of their families to succeed. These various expectations and preconceptions contribute to gender-specific risks of marginalisation of YMM. Counteracting the discrimination and marginalisation of YMM from non-European countries and implementing policies to support their well-being constitute significant European challenges. This paper looks at the experiences of young Kurdish and Turkish migrant men living in several European countries and their notions of wellbeing. It is part of the wider European project on "Migrant Men's Wellbeing in Diversity" which seeks to evaluate the experiences of YMM in different domains such as at school, at work, in the neighbourhood/community, with the authorities/families/peers with respect to notions of well-being.

***

SESSION 7A – Between Naturalization and Irregularity: Migrants and (Il)legal Membership in Turkey

Migration and Citizenship: The Case of Turkey

(42) Zeynep Kadirbeyoğlu (Boğaziçi University) and Dilek Çınar (Boğaziçi University)

Since the 1990s, the link between immigration and citizenship acquisition has been subject to an impressive body of national as well as comparative research projects conducted in different Western European countries. Turkey has been included in such studies as a major sending country and Turkish immigrants' attitudes towards becoming German, Dutch or Belgian citizens have attracted considerable attention by scholars of migration as well as of policy-makers. However, studies that focus on Turkey as a country of destination for international migrants are yet rare. Moreover, the few studies available focus rather on the historical trajectory of Turkish citizenship policy, while detailed research on the current citizenship legislation and particularly of its administrative implementation is still lacking. Still less attention has been paid to the subjective perspectives and motives of immigrants who have acquired Turkish citizenship or are intending to do so.

Filling this gap is the major aim of our ongoing research project that analyzes 1) the legal framework of Turkish citizenship policies; 2) the administration of applications for naturalization; 3) the motives and experiences of non-nationals on their way of acquiring Turkish citizenship. Furthermore, our argument is that Turkey provides a special and exciting case for comparative studies of citizenship policies for two reasons. First, having been for many decades a major country of emigration, Turkey had finally to find ways to accommodate the needs of Turkish citizens living abroad, e.g. the question of dual/multiple nationality, military service or (more recently) external voting rights for emigrants. In our presentation, we will discuss how in recent times Turkish citizenship law and policies have been amended in response to the needs of a large community of Turkish citizens living abroad. Second, piecemeal changes in legislation may appear as "bureaucratic technicalities" but such developments should be subject to (political) theoretical scrutiny as well. Thus, we will reflect upon recent changes in Turkish citizenship legislation with reference to broader current political science debates on "de-ethnicization"" vs. ""re-ethnicization" of the concept of (national) citizenship. Our argument is that both dynamics can and do go hand in hand.
***

Migration Policy and Migration Management of Syrians in Turkey

(40) Michelle Dromgold (Middle East Technical Universtiy)

In 2010, the number of migrants to Turkey surpassed the number of migrants from Turkey, signifying a shift in Turkey's historical trend as a migratory 'sending' country to that of a 'receiving' country as well. To address such changes, the national government issued the Law on Foreigners and International Protection (Law No. 6458) in April 2013 and establishment a new Directorate General of Migration Management. These changes signify a shift in the national government's practices and discourses on migration towards management of migration and an increased multilateral management of migration. However, the Turkish national government, its determination and implementation of migration policy remain at the core of this migration management system. It is such policies that outline the rights of migrants, the workings of NGOs and the involvement of the international community. With the influx of Syrians into the country in the last four years, Turkey must now additionally respond to migration in a new and unprecedented way. This paper outlines Turkey's legal policy of temporary protection under which Syrians are allowed to stay in the country. Based on data collected in thirty-one interviews conducted with NGOs and government employees in Ankara, Gaziantep, Istanbul, and Şanliurfa, this paper further outlines the critical problems resulting from the Syrian flows. Although the Turkish government has established legal provisions for Syrians' inclusion into Turkish society, Syrians remain excluded as 'guests' and are normalized as the 'other' in the country.

***

Dual Citizenship and Other Modes of Legal Membership in the Transnational German-Turkish Space: Notes from Turkey

(39) Barbara Pusch (Orient-Institut Istanbul)

Parallel to the worldwide globalization process and the consolidation of transnational spaces the question of dual legal inclusion and membership has gained importance. As transnational spaces are strongly determined by pluri-local and cross border practices of political, cultural and economic activities of a large variety of people, dual state membership is the "natural equivalent" (Faist 2000: 209) to these activities. However, within the German-Turkish context the necessary judicial reforms are lagging behind. While maintaining dual citizenship has been possible in Turkey since 1981 there is - despite all legal reforms - no general right to obtain dual citizenship in Germany. This has not only led to international critique of the German citizenship law but also influenced policies of Turkey. The Turkish invention of the Blue Card (formally referred to as Pink Kart) in 1995 has to be seen in this context. The result of all these legal developments is a highly diverse set of statuses according to which different groups of people are included legally in the transnational German space.

The proposed paper focuses on the various forms of multiple legal memberships in the transnational German-Turkish space. More specifically, the aim of the paper is to investigate the differences regarding the granting of dual German-Turkish citizenship and multiple memberships to German citizens of Turkish and non-Turkish origin in Turkey. By doing so the paper will explore the current legal framework and the legal practice within the wider context of German-Turkish relations, transnationalization, (dual) citizenship and multiple memberships from three perspectives: (1) the legal, (2) the socio-political and (3) the self-perspective of German citizens of Turkish and non-Turkish origin in Turkey. Since the regulations regarding dual citizenship and other forms of multiple membership are currently in flux (4) another aim of the project will be (4) to analyze the reforms introduced by the Law on Foreigners and International Protection in Turkey and (5) the reform of the so-called "option obligation" for migrants born to foreign parents in in order to shed light on the presently ongoing and future developments.

As the mainstream of research on German-Turkish transnationalization remained captive in "national containers" and mainly focused on the "German side" of this space, the "Turkish side" has largely been neglected. Therefore the paper will mainly focus on the implication of these reforms for people living on the "Turkish side" of this space.
***

Migrant Women's Labor, Gendered Morality and Law

(75) Ayşe Parla (Sabancı University)

This paper will explore the relationship between law and the gendered nature of migrant labor through a comparative analysis of how even the undocumented migrant bodies are hierarchized in the contemporary landscape in Turkey. I situate the predicament of Bulgarian Turkish women, who work predominantly in domestic work, against the backdrop of two recent tragedies involving undocumented migrants from other ethnic/national origins: the suicide of an Armenian migrant woman after being "shamed" by her fiancée, a Turkish citizen; and the murder of an Ugandan migrant woman after being raped by a acquaintance, again a Turkish citizen. After positioning these "killable bodies" within the larger context of anti-immigrant sentiment, sexism and informal work conditions in Turkey, I address what I call the "relative privilege" of Bulgarian Turkish migrant women, who occasionally benefit from the protection offered by the shield of ethnicity and religion as well as from periodic amnesties that enable legalization.

I present my argument through the dual filter of law and culture. Put differently, I explore the entanglements, between, on the one hand, the juridical system which "keeps up" with the wider, international legal regime of regulating migrant labor across Europe, and on the other hand, the specific manifestations and repercussions of such regulations as they are inflected by the particular cultural and familial norms in Turkey: the legal and cultural production of migrants as more or less "kin," as more or less absorbable within the nuclear (and national) family. I pay specific attention to the conditions that led to the 2012 revision to the Law on the Travel of Foreigners, which broadened the scope of the already existing regulation of the maximum 90 days of stay, as well as the subsequent concerted efforts to register and regularize the field of domestic labor through both facilitating and intensifying surveillance over work permit application procedures.

The end goal is not to propose a hierarchy of victimhood. Rather, I seek first to highlight important distinctions among migrant women often assumed to be equally vulnerable, or vulnerable in the same ways. And second, I show that even for those with relative privilege, social rights are far from secure within the current configuration of neoliberalism and conservatism, a regime that reinforces internal distinctions within the labor force both through law and through gendered morality.

***

SESSION 7B – Politics and Migration

External Voting: 2014 Presidential Elections of Turkey

(26) Nalan Soyarık Şentürk (Başkent University)

The presidential elections of 2014 in Turkey brought about critical changes in terms of the relations between the citizen and the state. First, the president was to be elected directly by the people for the first time in the republican history. Secondly, the emigrants from Turkey would be able to vote for the president in the countries they reside, again for the first time. This study will elaborate on the issue of external citizenship and voting rights, especially focusing on the 2014 presidential elections.

The rights and duties of those citizens who have migrated to and residing in another country are intriguing issues. As Bauböck states "the right to return and to diplomatic protection" are the two core rights of the external citizens. Some countries, also entitle the external citizens with the duty to pay taxes. In most cases, the question of political participation of the emigrants in the country of origin remains a question. Would they be entitled to vote or not? If so, how would the voting process be conducted?

In 2012 by a new law the migrants from Turkey were granted the right to vote in the designated embassies and consulates, in addition to customs at the borders. Previously, ballots could only be casted at the borders. The new amendment aimed at the improvement of the voting process for those citizens living and residing abroad. Keeping the ties close with the migrants had always been one of the aims of the Turkish governments. However, the changes in the voting process were introduced almost fifty years after the beginning of the migration process. This leads to the second set of questions this study intends to focus on. The Turkish understanding of citizenship is a republican understanding that endows the citizen with duties towards the state in return to which rights are gained. Thus, the republican understanding aspires for the participation of those citizens in a stated territory. However, extension of external voting rights challenges the republican principles. On the other hand, Turkey is becoming a migrant receiving country. Even though the legislation concerning foreigners and international protection is clarifying questions over residency and related rights, the question over the possibility of their participation in the political process remains intact.

This study aims at highlighting the discussion over political participation of the migrants in the Turkish context. A survey on the voting experiences of emigrants in the recent elections is planned to be conducted. The findings of the survey will contribute to the discussions over the meaning of citizenship, the rights of the citizens and the extent of the enjoyment of those rights. Finally, the study aims to contribute to understand the migratory process of Turkey.
***

Combatant or Civilian? Paramilitary Organizations in Turkey and International Humanitarian Law

(108) Ethem Coban (Goethe University Frankfurt)

Paramilitary organizations, particularly the Kontrgerilla (Counter Guerrilla), Köy Korucuları (Village Guards), and JITEM (Gendarmerie Intelligence Organization) played a multidimensional role in Turkey's younger history. These state-funded and equipped units were actively engaged in the Kurdish Conflict of Turkey at the side of the Turkish Armed Forces, while at the same time directly involved in the suppression of the civilian population targeting the mainly Kurdishinhabited southeast of the country. Judged by the number of grave human rights violations (extra-judicial killings, political assassinations and disappearances), and transnational crimes committed, critical research is deemed instrumental to a (post-) conflict society. Whereas a good quantity of research has been devoted on the Kurdish Conflict, a legal analysis from the standpoint of jus in bello (laws governing warfare) on deployed paramilitary organizations falls rather short. The scope of this research is to fill this gap.

Against this background, this paper will establish the legal status of the paramilitaries pursuant to International Humanitarian Law (IHL). As the legal status of conflict parties is dependent on either one of the two governing legal regimes – Additional Protocol (AP) I or II to the Geneva Conventions – two preconditions need to be fulfilled: (i) does the situation in southeast Turkey fulfill the requirement of an armed conflict pursuant to IHL? Although public opinion and academia tend to refer to the events as an armed conflict, the IHL threshold on the existence of an armed conflict is neither defined, nor uniform. (ii) If then, the situation amounts to an armed conflict, a classification as either international or non-international armed conflict is compelling. Turkey is neither signatory to AP I regulating international armed conflicts, nor AP II regulating non-international armed conflicts, as such the

question whether these regimes have risen to customary law needs further scrutiny.
***

Politically Motivated Migration: The Case of Turkish Migration to Northern Cyprus

(14) Yücel Kemal Vural (Eastern Mediterranean University), Başak Ekenoğlu (Eastern Mediterranean University) and Sertaç Sonan (Eastern Mediterranean University)

The increasing number of Turkish immigrants in the northern part of Cyprus and their influence in politics has become a sensitive and controversial issue both at intra-communal and inter-communal level of politics in Cyprus since 1974. While this has led to a fear of assimilation among some Turkish Cypriots, it prompted the Greek Cypriots who see these immigrants as settlers, to accuse Turkey of following a policy of colonization. Nevertheless, there is no official 'migration policy' employed by the government in the northern part of Cyprus. Indeed there have been public policies aiming at regulating the unexpected results of migration rather than identifying the preferred conditions of migration.

In the literature, 'political migration' has usually been associated with forced migrants such as refugees, displaced persons, etc. The case of northern Cyprus, however, seems to represent a distinct category where 'politically motivated migration' is a result of a combination of domestic policies of the host country and foreign policy objectives of the home country. Furthermore, different from the related literature that concentrates on the general economic or political reasons behind migration to 'economically developed' countries, this paper intends to analyze migration through classifying the reactions of a 'developing host country.' By focusing on three different waves of Turkish immigration, this paper argues that 'politically motivated' immigration has generated three different types of reactions in Turkish-Cypriot community. Namely, (1) clientelist reaction, which sees immigration from a nationalistic-opportunistic perspective; (2) protectionist reaction, which sees immigration as a threat to the Turkish-Cypriot identity and political stability; and (3) legalist reaction, which sees immigration as a human rights issue. The paper argues that there has been a distinct policy of 'clientelism' of the host country which overlaps with the home country (Turkey) foreign policy objectives which mobilized Turkish migration to northern Cyprus.

***

"Mental Health and Political Engagement in Context of Diaspora"

(84) Zübeyit Gün (Gediz University)

The place of resettlement of forced migrants is also the place where they carry their political struggles. It is observed that the sphere of political struggle is reproduced and reconstructed within the diasporas. The transfer and reconstruction of political thoughts, and therefore political activities, to the place of resettlement may have many effects at different levels and directions to the host country, migrants and migration groups.

The purpose of this study is to analyze how the development of post-traumatic stress disorder (PTSD) and acculturation processes of forced migrants are affected by their political engagement in the context of forced migration. The population represents Kurdish migrants who had forcibly migrated to France (Paris) after 1991. The relationship between PTSD, acculturation processes and political engagement is also analyzed according to gender differences. Qualitative researches methods were used for collecting data and for analyzing the collected data content analysis was used.

According to the results, political groups play important roles for Kurdish forced migrants at the beginning of their arrival. Political group is a protective factor for migrants' social and economic welfare, also for their mental health especially for the new comers. On the other hand, in the long run, due to the group dynamics, it turns out to be a retarding factor for the treatment of PSTD symptoms and is becoming a negative factor for migrants' acculturation process. It is also found out that engagement into a political group has different impact on women and men.

***

SESSION 7C – Integration and Identity

The integration of immigrants in rural communities: the case of Turks in France

(3) Marketa Seidlova (Charles University)

As one of the countries which have among the European ones the longest tradition in receiving immigrants, France is often studied for its experiences with integration of immigrants. This paper explores the un/success of adopted attitude on the example of Turkish community in the Basse-Normandy region in France.

The rural region of Basse-Normandy is known as the region with the lowest share of immigrants on total population in whole France (2 %). However, the half of immigrants in this region comes from 5 countries: Morocco, Portugal, Turkey, the United Kingdom and Algeria, when the immigrants from Turkey are – compared to the French average – overrepresented. Moreover, they represent even 41 % of immigrants in the city of Flers. Due to such high share on the immigrant population, the questions as

"Where do they come from? What brought them over there? What are they doing there?" come immediately on our minds.

These questions are answered with the help of field survey, which has been carried out between 2007 – 2011 and which gives us also the insight to the work of local governments of the city of Flers: what concrete measures did they use to support the integration of Turks into the everyday life of major society? The attitude of the city of Flers is then compared with the attitude of other cities in this region and also with the attitude of French government. the results shows that the Town halls in surveyed cities apply in the everyday practice a number of tools and measures which correspond with the multicultural model of local integration policy as defined by Alexander (2007). The policy measures of studied cities/districts towards immigrants was significantly influenced by the size of immigrant population, the duration of its presence in the city and its composition (country of origin, type of migration, etc.) and also by the political persuasion of the city leaders.

The data were obtained in semi-structured interviews with representatives of NGOs and of municipalities. Statistical data then shows to which extent these efforts were successful by comparing the main labor occupations of Turkish descents in both region of Basse-Normandie and in Paris, the economic capital of France.

Mapping Turkish minority media in Germany: Towards a more diverse diasporic mediascape

(67) Çiğdem Bozdağ (Kadir Has University)

Turkish labor migration in Germany has a history of over 50 years, so as the media addressing Turkish migrants in Germany. This paper discusses the developments in the history of Turkish minority media in Germany and argues that there is a diversification and increase of diasporic minority media produced by and for Turkish migrants in Germany by focusing on especially the internet era. On the one hand, the costs of media production and distribution decreased with the internet, which resulted in the increasing numbers of Turkish minority media. On the other hand, different generations of Turkish migrants in Germany have diverse cultural orientations, which are reflected in their diasporic media production.

First programs to address the Turkish population in Germany were the so-called guestworker radio shows, which were designed by the German public media services in the 1960s. These were followed by the Turkish newspapers from Turkey starting to sell their products to the Turkish population in Germany and German TV shows in the 1970s. These were mainly public-sector programs in Germany or commercial programs from Turkey. Especially towards the end of 1970s and beginning of 1980s, Turkish migrants started to produce their own media including films, newspapers and magazines. The first commercial Turkish TV and radio channels by migrants themselves were produced in the 1990s.

Digital technologies and the internet brought a new dimension to the diasporic mediascape in 1990s by enabling cheaper production and easier distribution of minority media. This resulted in the emergence of a high number of diasporic websites - including social network sites, gaming services, chat, blogs, news websites, discussion forums, video services - becoming available. This paper will firstly give a brief overview of historical developments in diasporic media production by Turkish migrants in Germany. Then, it will present a mapping of the online diasporic media on the basis of a media ethnographic analysis of Turkish diasporic websites, which includes observations, interviews and content analysis of the websites.

***

Diasporic Identities in Ethnic Community Football: Case of Turkish and Kurdish Leagues in London

(24) K. Onur Unutulmaz (Social Sciences University of Ankara)

Using the findings of a 1.5-year multi-sited ethnographic fieldwork centered in London, this

paper proposes to manifest that ethnic community football leagues constitute significant
transnational social spaces in which diasporic
identities are formed, negotiated, and reproduced.
As part of my doctoral research for the degree of
DPhil in Anthropology at University of Oxford, I
have conducted 72 in-depth interviews comple-
menting a wealth of ethnographic data collected
through participant observation, analysis of secondary sources as well as various archives.

I propose to present evidence to show that
the fear of 'losing the youth' to assimilation and
degeneration is a common and unifying concern
for the Turkish-speaking community in London.
I argue that this fear has been extremely influential in the creation of ethnic community football
as a field and has ever since functioned as the
most prominent factor motivating adults to get
involved. The different identity projects, I further
argue, formed as a result of communal negotiation, are reflections of the vision for how to
respond to this crisis.

In terms of gender identities, I argue that this
very same identity crisis is characterised as a 'crisis of masculinity', in at least a double sense,
which has found its manifestation in organisation
around an almost exclusively male site, where
hegemonic ethnic masculinities are negotiated
and produced. Here, I argue that the one defining
and unifying aspect of all the ethnic identities
reproduced within the field is their masculine

character. I show that these 'masculine ethnicities' or 'ethnicised masculinities', while reproduced in an almost exclusively male site, represent wider dynamics of the patriarchal structure of the community and the crisis of masculinity experienced in the diaspora.

The structure and position of the field of Turkish-speaking football, which is conveniently situated in the Turkish-speaking private and the British/Londoner public, has been an essential factor accounting for the effectiveness of this field for (re)producing, maintaining, transmitting, and representing hybrid masculine ethnic identities.

***

Place Attachment Effects of Urban Belonging on the Tendency to Migrate: Case of Zonguldak

(99) Hasan Sankır (Bülent Ecevit University)

There are crucial impacts of social and physical environments on identity process realized by people with different interactions. People's internalization of the physical and the social environment by using them, that is the appropriation of the environment, creates hegemony and this situation generates the feelings of belonging. In this sense, belonging to the space and urban consciousness cause people to questioning about where they belong in the process of their everyday interactions. Individuals do not feel themselves safe and do not feel belonged to that environment when they cannot create hegemony on the environment they live in.

Objectives: It is to demonstrate the impacts of city/resident relationship of people who have a tendency of migration from Zonguldak on their will to migrate. This relationship is evaluated in terms of urban consciousness and belonging.

Methods: A field study on the residents of Zonguldak was conducted to realize these aims of the research. A survey was applied to 1420 respondents in Zonguldak city center. There were 9 open-ended questions, 41 close-ended questions and a Likert scale consisting of 20 items; 70 questions in total in the questionnaire.

Results: It is found out that the degree of urban attachment varies according to certain criteria such as age, marital status, having children, level of education, income level, time spent in the city, ownership of the house, previous experience of migration and feeling belonged to the city. It is seen that within this context, the will to leave the city and migrate emerges.

Conclusion: The findings underscore association between tendency to migrate and urban consciousness. These associations highlights the need for social strategies such as improving social and physical environment.
***

SESSION 7D – Spatial Productions of the Social: Identity, Subjectivity and Power

Return without Going Back

(15) Joost Jongerden (Wageningen University)

The destruction and burning of thousands of rural settlements by the Turkish army and para-military forces and the forced migration of hundred thousands, if not millions of (mostly) Kurdish villagers has left a heavy legacy, socially, politically, and economically. Though much has been said about forced migration and the under-lying village evacuation and destruction, several issues remain unclear or undisclosed. In this contribution I will discuss socio-economic and demographic issues we should take into consideration when talking about return and return-to-village programs, such as the changing rural-to-urban population ratio, agricultural policies, the development of multi-place settlement patterns and the demography of return. Related to this, I will problematize the 'rights' approach (right-to-return discourse), which, as I will argue, does not protect and empower displaced persons, but surrenders them to the state. The challenge is to create new perspectives, new ideas, new ap-proaches to and maybe new solutions for a pressing problem that has not been properly faced within the context of the state and rights over the last few decades.

***

Home of the Kurdish Seasonal Workers as a Rural and Colonial Space

(22) İclal Ayşe Küçükkırca (Mardin Artuklu University)

The aim of this paper is to explore the gendered relations and transformations at the homes of the seasonal migrants leaving from Diyarbakır to pick hazelnuts in the Black Sea region in the post-1990 period. I conceptualize home as a space composed of both public and private aspects, constituted through a set of organized habitual and habituated spatio-temporal relations, produced by different subject positions. (Lefebvre, Bourdieu) Moreover, the homes of the female Kurdish seasonal migrants are formed in a rural context along with colonial conditions that effect the relations at home that are social, political or economic in character. Resting on anecdotal pieces that came out of an ethnographic study, the paper tries to make sense of the home of the female seasonal migrants in terms of its gendered, class or ethnic dynamics while exploring the tensions and transformations of the relations between the public and the private homes of Kurdish people. In turn, it will propose a link between the political power of the Turkish state and seasonal migration that shapes the private space of the Kurdish migrants. It will

conclude by claiming that the boundary between the public and the private realms change via gendered and ethnic lines for the Kurdish female seasonal workers, and both the private and the public is lost in the Black Sea region.
***

15 Year Record of the Municipal Practices of HADEP-BDP Line

(60) Ali Ekber Doğan (Mersin University)

Since 1999 local elections, an increasing number of cities is being governed by the cadres of HEP-DEP-HADEP line. For example, while HADEP won 37 settlements or cities (7 city center of provinces, 23 districts and 7 towns) in 1999 elections, under the name of BDP that political line raised this count to 110 (10 city center of provinces, 67 districts and 33 towns).

Since 1999, municipalities have been one of the most significant communication/ relation level for Kurdish political movement with local people. Beside this, empowerment of local governments have given a central role in Abdullah Öcalan's "democratic autonomy" solution for the "Kurdish Problem". Practices of those municipalities have been shaped by the pendulum between the hegemony of neoliberalism-Islamism as the municipal policies in Turkey) and the processes of clashes and negotiations between government and Öcalan/KCK or PKK.

In this presentation, I will try to make a critical evaluation of 15 years of municipalism experience of cadres from HADEP to BDP by the totality of their policies or practices. These years have been also known as the years of the empowerment of municipalities in the dimensions of local autonomy and fiscal resources. Is that empowerment carrying the potential of real solutions to the problems arised from identity and social-spatial problems?

In this paper, I will look for the questions listed below: How could those municipalities use those potentials?; What have been the potential obstacles emanating from the mentality and practies of municipalities; Has those municipalities been different from the hegemonic neoliberal-Islamist municipal policies (if there is, from which angles can we observe that difference); how could we define the municipal practice of HADEP-BDP line?

This study is mostly based on observations and municipal publications of the concerned cities. Besides, I will be also using works of other writers/researchers who consider the national struggle in combination with social-class liberation, with women's freedom and with preservation of nature.
***

Migrant Associations and Economic Integration. Example of Turkish, Sub-Saharan and Balkan Minorities in Belgium, Luxembourg and the Czech Republic

(2) Andrea Gerstnerova (IRFAM) and Altay Manço (IRFAM)

Associations of migrants are generally presented as platforms for meetings, information exchange and social networking. But they are also cultural identity holders and centres for altruistic help and solidarity. To some extent they even play the role of job-facilitators. This communication offers a broad insight into the intra-community life of the three non-EU communities residing in Luxembourg, the Czech Republic and Belgium. It shows as well the crucial factors for the development of a dynamic associative life that is essential for the smooth integration of immigrants in the local labour market.

In the context of the global economic crisis, the paper analyses the dynamics, basic functions, forms, limits and levels of efficiency of Sub-Saharan, Balkan and Turkish migrant associations. While, the majority of Sub-Saharan immigrants used to consider the associations as problem-solving mediators (get residence documents, send remittances to the family…), the Balkan and the Turkish immigrants used to take

them as a medium for their socio-cultural enter-
tainment and their economic integration.
However, the objectives of migrant associations
change in harmony with desires of their members
and pressing needs emerged either in the host
society, or in the country of origin…

The paper is based on the secondary analysis
of the previous scientific work conducted by
Manço (2006), Amoranitis and Manço (2011) and
Gerstnerova (2013) and the comparison of the
statistical data among selected countries.
***

Women across Borders: Daily Life Experi-
ences of Turkish Women in Belgium

(13) Latife Akyüz (Düzce University), Metin Kılıç
(Düzce University) and Hatice Esra Oğuz (Düzce
University)

Since 1960's, with the massive migration
movement of labour from the third world to
Europe, the migration process and the integration to the social, cultural and economic life of
received countries have taken significant importance in social science, specifically within
migration studies. Although it's been the third
generations living in those countries, the integration problems of migrants have been remained in
agenda. Taking this point to account, the aim of
this paper is understanding and discussing the
experience of women who migrated from Turkey

to Belgium in the way of integration process to economic, cultural and social life in the light of the migration and transnational families' studies.

According to the data obtained from Prime Ministry of Republic of Turkey Presidency For Turks Abroad and Related Communities, in Belgium , 194.368 (2011) people with only Turkish or double citizenship are registered in Brussels Embassy. Turks are the second most populated immigrant community after Moroccans and about half of this population is comprised of women. However, as Sahin (2009) and Oztan (2010) suggested, there is no adequate study to understand how women experience the migration processes. In migration studies, migration is seen as a masculine experience and similar sort of ignorance of women experience might be observed in the studies surveying migration to Belgium. Yet women have special significance in migration processes both as an part of it and as a maintainer of social and cultural ties within their communities in receiving countries. Thus, in this study, we examine daily life of women, the problems they face, their situation in the family, understanding of womanhood and routine life handling methods from their own narratives.

In this research, we investigate two sample groups by using qualitative research methods. The first group was consisted of women who migrated to Liege, Belgium due to marriage and the second group comprises women who were

born and raised in Belgium. 30 women in total
are interviewed in depth.
***

Combatting fraud as a disincentive of an un-intended economic migrant: a comparative of the direct Turkish model and the indirect Australian model

(24TP) Sherene Özyürek (Victoria University),
Rodger Fernandez (Victoria University)

The consequence of fraud, namely removal, under the new Turkish Law Article 54 of the *Law on Foreigners and International Protection* represents a quick deterrent approach that can be finalised, including review procedures in most cases within 30 days, the Turkish model (Republic of Turkey Ministry of Interior Directorate General of Migration Management [RTMIDGMM], 2013).[3] On the other hand, Public Interest Criteria 4020 used in Australian law, is a lengthy process that has not achieved its goal of deterring unintended economic migrants, the Australian model.

Turkey's new laws take a holistic approach to identifying the fraud, focusing on the resulting visa, permit or residency permit granted, whereas Australia's approach is in relation to scrutiny of individual documentation that are fraudulent

---

[3] Law on Foreigners and International Protection No. 6458.

provided in support of the visa application. Where Turkey and Australia do take the same approach is that they both adopt the concept of "bans" after detection of fraud (RTMIDGMM, 2013, p. 11).[4] Turkey tackles fraud with an immediate action for removal with swift review measures whereas Australia's approach entails a lengthy review that can take up to two years until a decision is finally determined (RTMIDGMM, 2013, p. 30).[5]

In this paper, by undertaking a quantitative analysis of retrospective data (2011-2014) of the Migration Review Tribunal (produced by the Australian Government), the authors attempt to provide an insight into previous attempts to combat fraud to understand future effectiveness of the recent changes in both Turkey and Australia, given that the effects of recent changes in 2014 are still in progress. The results substantiate the authors' contention that in contrast to the Turkish model, the Australian model does not deter economic migrants but rather is a procrastinating tool used to the advantage of the visa applicant to obtain experience for potential short-term and long-term gain on their pathway

---

[4] Law on Foreigners and International Protection No. 6458, Article 9; Migration Regulations (Cth) 1994, Schedule 4, item 4020.

[5] Law on Foreigners and International Protection No. 6458, Article 54, Migration Act (Cth) 1958, s5(9).

to permanent residency through an unintended pathway.

***

Migrant Women's Social Integration: The Case of Turkish Ethnic Economy in London

(20TP) Saniye Dedeoğlu (Muğla Sıtkı Koçman University), Serap Özen (Muğla Sıtkı Koçman University)

This paper presents an account of the interaction between gender, labour in the ethnic economy and the social integration of migrants into their host society. With particular reference to the Turkish community in Britain, it investigates the relationship between Turkish women's work and their position in British society by focusing on how ethnically based employment affects their capacity to become socially integrated in the dominant society. Sharing the basic premise of Floya Anthias, developed in Ethnicity, Class, Gender and Migration (1992), that the use of female kinship labour has even been considered a necessary 'building block' for the development of ethnic minority enterprises in Britain, my argument is that women's work in the Turkish ethnic economy has been central to its development and success, but that this work has resulted in the invisibility of women's economic contributions both to their households and to their community. Although the role and use of female labour has been seen as necessary for the development of ethnic minority enterprises in Britain, gender sensitive research, however, shows that ethnic economies do not necessarily support the professional advancement of women as much as they do for men and can keep them in a subordinate position, thus preventing their integration into the host society. It is proposed that female immigrant workers are 'generally captive by other relationships than that of a wage' (Panayiotopoulos 1996:455). The predominantly male-controlled, labour-intensive nature of many ethnic economies are marked by 'social structures which give easy access to female labour subordinated to patriarchal control mechanisms' (Phizacklea 1988:22).

The material presented here explores how women have been silent contributors to the expanding family-based establishment of the Turkish ethnic economy in Britain. It further shows how women's work in the ethnic economy and their role in social ties and networks on which this economy depends preclude their social integration within the wider society. The agency of women in maintaining community networks and representing ethnic/national identity has been essential in the establishment and success of the Turkish community, which places more emphasis on women's traditional gender roles as mothers and wives. In this framework, women are seen to be under the control of patriarchal

and ethnic ties of their community. Therefore, gender divisions and the family are seen as central in understanding the forms of settlement and the economic and social integration of a migrant group in Europe. Migrants' interaction vis-à-vis the internal cultural and social differentiations within the group and the wider structural, institutional and ideological processes of the country of migration are affected by the very form of gender and family structures (Anthias 1992).
***

SESSION 8B – Migrants of Istanbul

Expat Home-Making: A Discussion on Identities and Home-Making Practices in the Case of Expat European Women in Istanbul

(47) Didem Kılıçkıran (Kadir Has University)

In recent years, there has been a growing interest in the ways in which migrant identities are enacted in particular settings. Yet, there is still little research on the lives of contemporary 'expats' and on how they construct sites of identity, of home and belonging. 'Home', as both a space of everyday experience and imaginary belonging (Blunt and Dowling, 2006), is particularly problematic with respect to expats as they are widely seen as individuals who prioritize mobility over attachment, unlike immigrants and refugees from the underdeveloped parts of the world for whom the quintessential paradox of migration – that it brings about an ever greater need for a place-based attachment – is a reality that shapes everyday lives. This seems to be a viable explanation for why expats have been largely excluded from the interdisciplinary studies on migration and mobility which is increasingly enriched by detailed analyses of the materialization of the need to belong.

In this paper, I aim to discuss the results of my ongoing ethnographic research in which I examine the home-spaces of European expat women in Istanbul in relation to the representation and renegotiation of identities. Drawing on in-depth interviews, I discuss the meanings expat women attach to their new lives in Istanbul, their memories of the places they left behind, the habits and aspects of material culture they have carried from those places, and everyday practices through which they construct the boundaries of their private lives, in order to show the ways in which they transform their domestic spaces into home-places. I suggest that there are as much continuities as ruptures unveiled in these spaces, and that 'home' as a material site of identity and belonging still matters to expat women however much they value mobility and change.
***

Greek migrants in Istanbul

(113) Georgia Mavrodi (European University Institute)

Migration scholars treat Turkey as a country of emigration, as a transit route, and more recently as a country of settlement of migrants from Eastern Europe, the Middle East and Africa. By contrast, the study of the movement and settlement of EU nationals of non-Turkish descent often escapes attention. In the proposed paper we deal with the migration and settlement of Greeks in Istanbul since the year 2000 and we examine the reasons the Turkish metropolis has become an appealing destination for them as well as the extent to which personal and family migratory histories, past population movements and the legacy of conflict between the two countries influence their choices for migration and settlement. Finally, we are interested in those people's perceptions and beliefs about Turkey and the changes that may have taken place as a result of their settlement and life there. To this end, we use the results of a specially designed online survey conducted in 2013 and 2014.

***

Child-Rearing Practices within Mixed European-Turkish Families in Istanbul: Setting Symbolic Boundaries

(89) Nevena Gojkovic Turunz (İstanbul Şehir University)

The proposed article is a part of a wider research on mixed European-Turkish families residing in Istanbul. Although the creation of a new family always involves 'imagining', mixed couples necessarily answer more abstract questions than mono-cultural: a) Who are we as a family and where do we stand vis-a-vis our respective societies?; b) Who are our children going to be in terms of ethnic and religious belonging? c) How we will raise them?. This article is focused on the third question: the child rearing practices within mixed families. The objective is twofold. First, it examines the perceptions of foreign parents towards child-rearing practices of the Turkish society. Second, it examines the aims in child-rearing and cultural transmission of foreign parents. The article is based on 10 in-depth interviews conducted in Istanbul, followed by thick description. The results show that foreign parents tend to draw precise symbolic boundaries (Lamont) between their own and Turkish society in regard to children rearing practices and values associated with it. The boundaries are primarily created around the issues of education, the concept of a good mother, the role of extended

family, and specific values (e.g independence vs. dependence of children; hierarchical vs. egalitarian intergenerational relations).
***

Construction of ethnic identity among young Kurdish voluntary migrants in Istanbul

(79)Karol Kaczorowski (Jagiellonian University)

The aim of the presentation is to present partial results of ongoing research project devoted to examining ethnic identity of young Kurdish voluntary migrants in Istanbul. According to the research carried out by Rüstem Erkan in 2009 Istanbul is the province with the largest Kurdish population in the world. Moreover, Istanbul is of great significance for the Kurdish culture, as many Kurdish organizations were functioning in the city since the 19th century and many are active in 21st century. Analyses of internal migration in Turkey usually concentrate on problem of internally displaced people and force migration during 80's and 90's. However since the ceasefire with PKK in the following years, in 21st century voluntary migrations may constitute another wave of migration. Presented project aims at including in the scope of the research three combined areas that are related to creation of ethnic identity. The first area is understanding of Kurdish ethnic identity, and how young Kurds who have migrated to Istanbul make use of its patterns and dispositions during every day practices and social interactions. The second area covers history of migration to Istanbul, whereas the third area presents attitude of respondents towards multiculturalism of the city, how they perceive this phenomenon from the perspective of the Kurdish culture, and what's their contribution to the Istanbul community. For the purpose of the project cultural identity is understood as socially constructed, relative and processual as theorized by Frederik Barth, Stuart Hall and Thomas Hylland Eriksen. Construction of collective identity described by Shmuel Eisenstadt and Bernhard Giesen is also a theoretical framework of the study. Presented findings will base on 50 semi-structured interviews with Young Kurdish migrants from different districts in Istanbul.

SESSION 8C – Migration and Literature

From the Pen of an Immigrant Writer Murat Tuncel It Was Blue at the Palace of Justice and Shadow Girl

(121) Ayla Kaşoğlu (Gazi University)

When immigrant Literature is concerned, less interest is shown to the works of Turkish writers in Netherlands compared to Germany. One of these writers is Murat Tuncel who went to Netherlands in 1989 to teach Turkish lessons and is still continuing living there.

Tuncel who is not very well known in our country and has not any known study on his works in academic context was awarded with the Şükrü Gümüş Novel Award in 1994 for his work *Blue was the Palace of Justice* and Orhan Kemal Story Prize 2000, for *Shadow Girl* in which he deals with the case of emigration. Among his works which are translated into various languages *Blue was the Palace of Justice*, was translated into Dutch with the title *False Hope* in the years 2003-2004 (*Valse Hoop*).

In *Blue was the Palace of Justice* and *Shadow Girl*, reasons pushing immigrants/refugees beyond the border, existence in the places they went to, and struggle to survive is narrated with a stunning and realistic language. The hard part of being a foreigner, not knowing the language, fear of not receiving a residence permit, as well as homesickness and yearning for one's family, attitude towards the emmigrant in the neighborhood is put to the fore. In both works, unbreakable ties between people heading from Anatolia to Netherlands and Anatolian, their tiny worlds, how these worlds are exploited over time are transferred with delusion, associations and feedback. In *Blue was the Palace of Justice*, in Den Haag (the Hague), the city which distributes Justice to the world, justice does not reach these emigrants and is feared that it will never reach them. *In Shadow Girl* which consists of different stories, fears, troubles, anxieties and nightmares

are articulated after migration. In this presentation Tuncel's attitude on the issue of migration
will be examined with   an eclectic method.
***

Lost Ground: A Story of Migration from the Pen of Murat Işık

(124) Nazlı Gündüz (Gazi University)

Even though the place arrived for better opportunities and living conditions enables a person
feel excitement and fear simultaneously, his life
experiences, moral values and traditions are to
survive in memory and imagination during the
whirlpool of adaptation to that place.
Sometimes they want to keep these alive by passing them over to friends, children and
grandchildren. Sometimes the new location is
liked and adaptation occurs smoothly. With the
need of belonging to a social group, race and
religion, one inevitably gets stuck between the
new and old place, has adaptation troubles and
suffers difficulty, cannot accommodate oneself to
the new life and clings to the brought over language, traditions and culture.

This paper discusses the novel Lost Ground
written in Dutch (Verloren Grond) by Murat Işık,
a young author of Turkish origin, who at five
witnessed immigration from Turkey to Holland.
The novel was awarded with the best first novel
prize in Holland and the press depicted it as 'a

beautifully stunning family story'. Then, it returned homeland with its translation into Turkish (Kayıp Toprak). The narrator and protagonist is the child Mehmet Uslu who is forced to emigrate with his family. The plot consists of a tragic mutilation of a father, his family, experiences and a forced emigration from Sofyan to another village Hemgin and finally to İzmir. We closely witness their struggles in wastelands, the challenges of emigration and adaptation to new places, and poor living conditions.

The paper analyzes 'internal migration' in both books comparatively from a sociocultural view point within the perspective of sociology of literature.

***

Nazmi Adali'nin Feryatlarım Gözyaşlarım Adli Şiir Kitabında Göç Olgusu

(58) Aynur Özgür (Trakya University) and
Cengiz Tüsgil (Trakya University)

Yüzyıllar boyunca Türk ve Bulgar halkı aynı coğrafyada hatta aynı çatı altında barış içinde yaşamışlardır. Günlük hayattan kültüre, edebiyata kadar birçok alanda alışverişte bulunmuşlar ve birbirlerinden etkilenmişlerdir. Bulgaristan'da yaşayan Türkler nasıl Bulgarlardan etkilenmişlerse Bulgarlar da aynı oranda Türklerden etkilenmişlerdir. Özellikle edebi eserlerde bu etkinin izleri oldukça fazladır.

Çoğu göç tanımında, göçe sebep olan ortak noktaların siyasi ve ekonomik sebepler olduğu görülmektedir. 1989 göçünde de Türkler, Bulgaristan'dan siyasi sebepler dolayısıyla göç etmeye zorlanmışlar ya da kendi istekleriyle göç etmişlerdir. Bulgaristan Türklerinden olan Nazmi Adalı da, *"Feryatlarım Gözyaşlarım"* adlı şiir kitabında 1978 ve 1989'daki zorunlu göçü her yönüyle ele almıştır.

Şiirlerde göç sırasında yaşananlar tüm çıplaklığı ile gözler önüne serilmiştir. Göç sonrası geride kalanlara duyulan özlem, vatansızlık ve bir yere ait olmama duygusu belirli imajlar etrafında sade ama etkileyici bir dille anlatılmıştır. Bu çalışmada da imajlar doğrultusunda göç olgusu şiirlerde her yönüyle incelenmeye çalışılacaktır.
***

SESSION 8D – Identity in Kurdish Migration

Ethnolinguistic Repression of Kurds: a Narrative Ethnography

(38) Mediya Rangi (The University of Melbourne)

This presentation suggests an alternative approach for investigating the direct impacts of extensive, continuous, and long-term repression of Kurdish people: the largest state-less nation to date, discriminately divided across Central and Western Asia and dispersedly exiled into diaspora. As a result of the direct and indirect colonization experiments of the WWI allies, Kurdistan was divided across the territories now belonging to the handcrafted nation-states of Iran, Iraq, Turkey, Syria, and Armenia. These sovereignties continue to deny and repress Kurdish identity and political cultural expressions by violent genocidal means. Though the Kurdish studies literature is rapidly expanding, a more personal approach to investigating the permanent outcomes of ethnic repression against Kurds is required to go beyond the macro structural focus on political formations and movements. This project is a narrative ethnography that explores the personal subjective reality of experienced violence. It does so by creating a space for Kurds' voices to be heard through the most fundamental and basic form of human communication: storytelling, where Kurdish residents of New Zealand and Australia narrate their life experiences that led to their forced departure. As a fresh empirical extension to current literature, this project explores the sanctioned linguicide and ethnocide of an ethnolinguistic group who continue to find alternative ways to assert their identity and protect their linguistic, socio-cultural rights even in their exiled experience. Through a co-constructed and active methodology, this socio-anthropological research utilizes open narratives to document and understand the lived experiences of struggle and survival. These narrations provide a powerful account of two generations of Kurds' personal perseverance and determination, and assist in constructing a broader picture of their future as a collective ethnic community beyond borders.

***

As If All Life Had Vanished... The Return of Kurdish Villagers to Their Hometowns

(48) Şemsa Özar (Boğaziçi University)

My presentation will be about the return of Kurdish villagers to their hometowns. I will talk about those villagers who had been forced to flee their villages, in the early 1990s, in the course of the armed conflict between the Turkish security forces and the PKK (Partiya Karkerên Kurdistan – the Kurdistan Workers' Party). After living in Istanbul for almost a decade, in a metropole that they had no initial intention to settle, Kurdish villagers decided to go back to their homeland, to those villages they once had been brutally driven out of. I will first go back to the 1990s and briefly talk about the forced migration of Kurds and then I'll give a brief overview of the years spent in Istanbul. Then, I will try to demonstrate the struggle given to reestablish a life in the once brutally demolished villages.

It is well known that the majority of Kurds forced out of their homelands have not yet returned to their villages and homes. In this paper, I will rely on visual material and face-to-face interviews conducted with the returnees in the villages of Kavar, a region in the southwest of Lake Van, Behra Wanê (Van Sea) as Kurds name it.

Needless to say, the challenges and problems faced by the villagers during this whole fleeing and coming back home along with their perseverance in rebuilding a life and a community in their hometowns had, among other factors, revealed the political and ethical nature of their subjectivity vis-á-vis the Turkish state. This paper particularly aims to disclose the ways in which the Kavar people through all these years of struggle constructed their subjectivities expanding on political and ethical imaginaries.
***

Interregional Migration and Language Shift among Turkey's Ethnic Kurds

(151) Sinan Zeyneloğlu (Gaziantep University), Ibrahim Sirkeci (Regent's Centre for Transnational Studies) and Yaprak Civelek (İstanbul Arel University)

This study examines interregional migration and language shift among Turkey's Kurdish population using the 2000 Census data. First, we show that there is a language shift among the Kurds. Secondly, we map out the interregional migration patterns of Kurdish population in Turkey. For this purpose, instead of using on language data, which is not available for the last five decades through censuses, we preferred the birth region as an ethnic marker. This allows us factoring in possible language shift and assimilation. Our findings are presented in cross-tabulations using the variables age, gender, education, birth place, and place of residence. We have mapped the internal mobility by birth regions as well as language concentration across Turkey highlighting Kurdish and Arabic as common language in certain Eastern and Southeastern provinces.

Understanding Empowering Effects of the Kurdish Diaspora on Women's Agency: An Ontological Paradox

(112) Berivan Erbil (University of Gothenburg)

This article examines the gendered impacts of political and socioeconomic structures of the Kurdish Diaspora by reviewing the focus on the emancipatory effects of the diaspora on women's agency in the existing literature which overlooks the class and consciousness differences among these women. It is argued that despite the opportunity to acquire empowerment, most of Kurdish women are actually double-trapped by the polarisation between the homeland politics and host country politics. Based on the previous feminist-transnational studies on Kurdish women, the paper firstly discusses how their apparent empowerment can be misleading not only in their private spheres (in their family relations) but also in the public (at schools, workplaces etc) considering their vulnerable positions like being 'the disadvantaged other women' that substantially obscure their full participation, hence their personal gains, in the grassroots feminist movements. It further demonstrates that how the empowerment they gained can indirectly disempower them creating self-imprisoning identities through the diaspora's promise of ontological security for their ethnicity that pushes their gender-related problems into the background.

PLENARY SESSION C: Göç ve Edebiyat

Türk Göç Yazını Üzerine Bir Bakış

(28TP) Ali Tilbe (Namık Kemal University/Regent's University London)

Kökleri çok eskilere uzanan göç ya da sürgün olgusu, özellikle içinde bulunduğumuz çağın en sorunsal konularından birisi olarak ortaya çıkmaktadır. Göç eden insanları, yeni yaşamlarında çeşitli sorunlar beklemektedir. Göçmenler, özellikle ulusötesi göçmenler, öncelikle dil/iletişim sorunu başta olmak üzere, iki dillilik (Eng. bilingualism) kimlik (Eng. identity), ekinsel parçalanma (Eng. cultural fragmentation), toplumsal uyum (Eng. social harmony), bütünleşme (Eng. integration), yabancılaşma (Eng. alienation) gibi sorunları deneyimlerler. Bu sorunları aşmakta zorlanan göçmenlerin, çoğunlukla bir iyelik, yabansılık, yoksunluk ya da dışlanmışlık duygularına kapıldıkları görülür. Dil dışında, benzer sorunlar kuşkusuz içgöçler için de geçerlidir. Yeni uzamlarına alışmaya ve uyum sağlamaya çalışan insanların en büyük sıkıntısı, orada karşılaşacakları insanların ekinleri ve yaşam biçimlerini tanımamalarının ve geleceklerine ilişkin umutlarının gerçekleşip gerçekleşmeyeceğini bilememeleridir. Bütün bu olaylar, göçmenlerde kimi zaman bir başkaldırı ve reddetme duygusuyla içe kapanmaya, kimi zaman da bir bütünleşme ya da benzeşime yol açar. Bu duyguların anlatımını bulduğu en önemli alanlardan birisi kuşkusuz yazın ve sanat uzamıdır. Göçlerle birlikte, göçmen toplumların içinden çıkan yazar, düşünür ve sanatçı gibi aşkın özneler, bu yeni yaşam uzamlarında, toplumsal belleği ve ortak olası en üst bilinci en iyi biçimde yansıtmayı başarabilen özgün sanat, müzik ve yazınlarını yaratmaktan geri kalmamışlardır. Türk göçüne yönelik bu yeni yaratı alanı da, eleştirmenlerce göç, sürgün, göçmen ya da konuk işçi yazını gibi değişik adlandırmalarla anılmış ve göç ile yazın ilişkisi bu araştırmalarda ilgi odağı olmaya başlamıştır. Gerek ülkemizde gelişen iç göç odaklı göç yazını, gerekse de Almanya, Fransa ve öteki

Avrupa ülkelerinde Türkçe yapıtlarıyla tanınan Nedim Gürsel gibi Türkiye kökenli yazar ve şairimizin yarattığı bir göçmen/sürgün yazını söz konusudur. Bunun yanında Belçika'da doğup büyüyen ve yapıtlarını Fransızca yazan Kenan Görgün gibi yeni kuşak yazarlar, yaşadıkları ülkelerin dillerinde yetkin yapıtlar vermektedirler. Biz, bu bildiride, Türk göç olgusunun yazın alanını daha çok izleksel bağlamda etkilediği varsayımından yola çıkarak, kısaca göç olgusunun genel çerçevesini belirledikten sonra, göç ve yazın ilişkisi üzerine kuramsal yaklaşımlardan söz edip, kimi ulusal ve ulusötesi düzeyde tanınan göç romanı yazan ve göçmen yazarlar ile yapıtlarından örneklerle bu varsayımımızı açımlamayı erek ediniyoruz.
***

İki arada bir deredeki Türk'ün iç çekişi

(200) Nedim Gürsel (CNRS)

Yazmak, yalnızlaştıran bir deneyimdir. Beyaz sayfa, bir lambanın yalın aydınlığında Mallarmé'nin başını döndüren o yalnızlığı, yani bu korkunç düşünceyi dayatır. O, bu zorluğu ancak lambayı kendisinden uzaklaştırarak aşabilmiştir: "karanlık bir alan üzerine, parlak bir biçimde yazı yazılmaz". Kendi deyimiyle "kendisi yazından başka şey olmayan" Kafka, Felice'ye eşsiz tasarısından söz eder: yazmak için gerekli olan ne varsa alıp, ıssız geniş bir mahzenin ortasına bir lamba ile yerleşmek. "Yazarken asla yeterince yalnız olmayız" der, "yazarken çevrenizde asla yeterince sessizlik olmaz, gece yeteri kadar gece değildir".

***

Arafta Üretilen Yazınsal Metinler (göçmen türküleri, mektupları, öykü ve roman örnekleri)

(54) Füsun Bilir Ataseven (Yıldız Teknik University)

II. Dünya Savaşı'nın yarattığı ekonomik bunalımdan sonra Avrupa ekonomisi kalkınmaya başladığında yeni iş gücüne duyulan ihtiyaç, çeşitli ülkelerden sağlanmaya çalışıldı.1960'lı yıllarda önemli miktarda işçi, geçici bir süre için gittiklerini düşünerek ülkelerinden göçtüler.

Göçmek eylemi TDK Türkçe Sözlüğünde, "kendi ülkesinden ayrılarak yerleşmek için başka ülkeye giden (kimse, aile veya topluluk)", "bir ülkeden bir başka ülkeye yerleşmek amacıyla giden kişi, aile ya da toplumsal küme" ve "genellikle yerleşmek amacıyla, bir yerleşim yerinden bir başka yerleşim yerine, bir ülkeden bir başka ülkeye gitme eylemi" gibi hiçbir kötü, ayrımcı veya ırkçı anlam içermeyen ve "yerleşme" tasavvurunu içinde barındıran bir kavram olarak verilmektedir.

Yazınsal ifade ise insanın varoluş sorununun çevirisidir, dışa vurumudur. Dil seçimi yazarda içsel, kimliksel ve ruhsal gerilimi gösterir. Yazar için dilsel seçim kimliksel bir göstergedir, ötekinin dilinde yazmak ister ideolojik ister sembolik olsun, bir çeşit yabancılaşma ve ihanet gibi algılanabilir, içsel acıların ve gerilimlerin belirtisidir. Çok dilli bireyler, kullandıkları ve kimliklerinin bir parçasını oluşturan dillere bağlılık duymaktadırlar.

Homi Bhabha, "üçüncü boyut" olarak tanımladığı kültür boyutunu aşan ve yeni bir boyuta taşınan bir oluşumdan söz ederek tamamen farklı, yeni bir şey üretildiğini vurgulamaktır. Bhabha'ya göre bir insanın kimliği, oluşum sürecinde kökeni sayesinde değil, farklılıkları algılayıp irdelemesi sayesinde oluşmaktadır. Bu kuram çerçevesinde, yeni üretilen eserler hem okuyucuları provoke etmeli, onlara yeni bir bakış açısı kazandırmalıdır (Hofmann, 2006). Bu çerçevede günümüzde "Kültüraşırı" veya "Kültürlerarası" kavramıyla tanımlanan edebiyat iki kültürü de kapsayan, yeni bir "üçüncü boyut" olarak anlaşılmaktadır.

Bu araştırmada söz konusu edilen göçmenlerin yarattıkları metinlerden yola çıkarak okura yansıyan çok dilliliği ve çok kültürü anlamaya çalışmak hedeflenmektedir. Seslerini duyurmaya ve kültürler arası bir iletişim kurmaya çalışan göçmenlerin özellikle ilk kuşağının seslenişlerini yansıttıkları türkülerinde yaşadıkları "kültür şoku" anlamak; daha sonraysa uyum sağlamaya çalıştıkları kültürde eleştirel bakıp haklarını arayan melez göçmenlerin mektuplarından yansıyan melez dile yoğunlaşmak gerekecektir.

***

Günümüzde Göç Edebiyatı Nedir?

(123) Seza Yılancıoğlu (Galatasaray University)

XX. yüzyılın ikinci yarısı, siyasal ve ekonomik koşulların getirdiği zorunluluklardan dolayı göç ve sürgün olaylarına tanık olur. Bu iki toplumsal dinamik; gelişmekte olan ülkelerden sanayileşmiş toplumlara doğru bir yöneliştir. Bilindiği gibi, Batı Avrupa'da özellikle Almanya'da iş gücü eksikliği ve Türkiye'nin ekonomik koşullarının getirdiği kısıtlamalar, Türkiye'den önemli bir iş gücünün Batı'ya göçmesine neden olur.

1960'lı yıllarda özellikle Almanya'ya doğru başlayan göç daha sonraki yıllarda Fransa, Belçika, İskandinav ülkelerine de yayılır. 1971 askeri muhtırasının ve 1980 askeri darbesinin ardından bu göç olayına zorunlu ya da gönüllü olmak üzere bir de sürgün durumu eklenir.

Bugün 1960'lı ve 1970'lı yılları göz önünde bulundurursak 40-50 yıl gibi aşağı yukarı yarım asırlık bir süreci arkada bıraktık. "Edebiyat toplumun aynası" olduğuna göre bu süreç Türk Edebiyatı'na nasıl yansıdı? Bugün halen "göç edebiyatı" ya da "sürgün edebiyatı" gibi tanımları kullanabilir miyiz ve nasıl kullanabiliriz?

Günümüzde Göç Edebiyatı nedir? başlıklı bildirimde, Kenan Görgün ve Sevgi Özdamar'ın yazınlarında, yaşadıkları göçün yapıtlarındaki uzantısını irdelemeye çalışacağım.

Bu yazarlar ile Nedim Gürsel yazını arasındaki benzerlik ve farklılıklara değinilerek "göç edebiyatının" bugünkü durumu tartışılacaktır.
***

SESSION PSD – Class-Formation and Urban Transformation

Spatial Segregation and Politics of Equilibrium in Mersin: Unintended Consequences of Forced Migration

(18) Bediz Yılmaz (Mersin University)

This paper will can be read as an attempt to answer the following question: starting from the second half of the 90s and throughout the 2000s (i.e. after the forced migration flow to the city), had a negative and full-of-tension city image to the outsiders to the extent that it was depicted as a "time-bomb, but why did Mersin not "explode"? I will try to build my analysis on four intricately related issues:

-spatial concentration which emerged as an unintented consequence of forced migration, that is, as a consequence of eviction without resettlement;

-the socio-historical background of Mersin as a city of migrations that has't got any native people;

-the informality as a source of mobility beyond subsistence activities within the vibrant economy of the city;

-inevitable regime of local politics working on a fragile basis of equilibrium.

By discussing these dimensions, I hope to be able to get a clearer image of the city of Mersin in relation to the forced Kurdish migration, not only in its socio-economic impacts (class formations and transformations) but also in the production and reproduction of urban space.

***

The Continuing Relevance of Class Analysis in Understanding Kurdish Migration: Theoretical and Methodological Considerations

(21) Cenk Saraçoğlu (Ankara University)

This paper aims to engage in a theoretical discussion as to the ways in which class analysis helps to understand the social and political ramifications of Kurdish migration into big cities in Turkey in the last twenty years. It is unequivocal that the course and the dynamics of Kurdish migration are intricately related to the ethnopolitical conflict experienced in Turkey since the early 1980s. Yet, this fact does not exclude the significance and necessity of class analysis in attaining a thorough understanding of multidimensional nature of Kurdish migration. At this point, however, one needs to clarify what it means to apply class analysis to the studies of Kurdish migration. This paper asserts that class analysis of Kurdish migration does not only include treating the individual class positions of Kurdish migrants as a variable shaping their conditions and experiences before and after migration. It also includes an analysis of how class relations in Turkish capitalism in general became constitutive of the social and economic context in which Kurdish migration took place. This perspective points to the necessity of bringing into focus the urban strategies of Turkish capitalism which appeared in the last twenty years as a vital component of the sustainability of capital accumulation. Such a perspective is the crucial first step to the analysis of Kurdish migration since the socio-economic and spatial transformation of Turkish cities in accordance with the necessities of neoliberal capital accumulation in Turkey constituted the structural basis of migration and thereby mediated the Kurds' experiences in the cities. The issue of Kurdish migration in this respect also includes the reactions and strategies that Kurdish migrants develop in the face of rapidly changing urban social context and class relations embedded in this rapid change. This paper will try to build this theoretical perspective on the basis of the findings of some fieldwork studies of the researchers conducted either in such big cities in Kurdish region as Diyarbakır or in Western metropolises as Istanbul and Izmir. As such, the paper will also yield an overall theoretical elaboration of the recently growing literature on Kurdish migration in Turkey.

***

Waiting for Investments: The Out-Migration of Business Classes from Diyarbakır

(44) Ayşe Seda Yüksel (University of Vienna)

Migration studies are mostly destination-oriented: they follow migrants' routes and examine the migrants in destination cities and urban markets. This study rather focuses on the departure site of migration and examines the out-migration waves from Diyarbakır, the symbolic and cultural center of Kurds in the Kurdish region of Turkey. Through the lens of an ethnographic research between 2007-2009, the study focuses on business classes in the city and investigates the narratives in the local market regarding the out-migration of business classes. The local economy of Diyarbakır has been shaped by asymmetrical migration waves (the out-migration of upper middle classes from the city and the inflow of Kurdish peasants that were internally displaced by the Turkish state) and characterized by high unemployment rates, stagnancy in commercial activities, and weak industrialization. In this stagnant economy, investment has become a magical word that conjures up urban development, and economic growth in the narratives of business people. In these narratives, the out-migration of business people is still one of the main referents in defining the contours of the local market. The city is put in a period of "waiting" for state subsidies and/or for external investors that mostly refer to the business people who migrated from the city since the 1960s. Their non-existence generates varying stories and disrupts the idea of an imagined community based on ethnic ties and co-locality. It is not only situated within a discourse of 'nostalgia' for the old times of Diyarbakır but also suspense and tension about the present and the future of the city. How did the out-migration shape the local economy in the 1990s? What are the recurring motifs in the narratives of business people regarding their peers that left the city? How are these motifs related to the ways business people remember the recent past of the city and the ways they construct their local identities within the local market?

***

Business and politics in Diyarbakır: An inter-elite adaptation in the changing political climate?

(56) Onur Öztürk

Since 2003, we have witnessed a rapid growth of the export-oriented manufacturing and service industries in Diyarbakır. At the same period, the local businesspeople have begun to uphold their own business agenda aloud, to take on active political roles and to gain importance in the inter-elite equilibria of the city. But they gained more visibility in particular with their active and unconditional support for "the peace process", arguing that they need a secure, peaceful Kurdish region to carry on economic activities.

While the Kurdish political elites and businesspeople have essential political contradictions between each other, these two groups maintain a common agenda at a local level: Sharing similar concerns on the topics like unemployment, economic development, urbanization etc., they continue to cooperate actively in the local governmental and non-governmental institutions around the values like citizenship, Kurdishness, an inter-elite sense of responsibility for the city of Diyarbakır.

However, the recent brutal rise of the Islamic State (IS) has dramatically changed the political climate of the region. AKP's disappointing policies concerning the war on IS and the Kurdish resistance against IS influenced and mobilized the local businesspeople in Diyarbakır who have lost abruptly much of their trade linkages in the conflict-affected areas and faced dramatic decreases in business volumes. Throughout this process they established closer cooperation and interaction with Kurdish political elites and thus, these two groups have begun to show a sort of mutual adaptation at a local level.

In this paper, I will discuss why and how these two elite groups, both subject to the same hegemony struggle going on between the AKP and the PKK, embark on a quest of mutual adaptation in Diyarbakır and which expectations and concerns do they have reciprocatively along these adaptation efforts. For this aim, I'm planning to analyze the development of the Organized Industrial Zone and to interview businesspeople and the Kurdish political elites in Diyarbakır.

***

SESSION 9A – Public Opinion and Syrian Movers

Local perceptions on Syrian migration to Turkey: A case study of Istanbul neighbourhoods

(34) Deniz Genç (Bahçeşehir University) and Merve Özdemirkıran (Bahçeşehir University)

Since the beginning of the crisis in Syria in March 2011, the number of Syrians crossing into Turkey has increased dramatically. Though most of the Syrian asylum-seekers are reported to live in those cities, where the camps have been set up, they are now almost in every city of Turkey. Among these cities, Istanbul hosts the largest number of Syrians. As their number increases, they become more visible and negative protests against them and incidents have been reported to take place.

Sharing the findings of an ongoing research on foreign policy choices and local actors, this paper takes a look at the mass migration of Syrians to Istanbul from the lowest level of administrative unit, from the neighborhood – Mahalle. The paper aims to answer two main questions: How do the Istanbulites perceive mass migration of Syrians to Turkey and to their neighborhoods and why do they have these perceptions? Secondly, the paper seeks answers to the questions of how this migration is absorbed by the neighborhoods in Istanbul and how it is being handled by the local authorities, Mukhtars.

The paper is built on the in-depth interview notes with 52 Mukhtars from 4 counties with the largest number of Syrian settlers - Fatih, Bahçelievler, Başakşehir and Gaziosmanpaşa. The data of the study is collected from the Mukhtars. Firstly because as they have to be the residents of the neighborhoods they are elected for, they are part of the public opinion of these neighborhoods. Moreover, they are in direct relationship with all the inhabitants, the locals and the Syrians and according to the Law No. 5393/2005 on Municipality, they are "authorized to declare opinion on the matters, which concern the neighborhood" (Law No. 5393/2005 on Municipality). With the primary data it presents, the paper is believed to

provide a fresh insight into the Syrian migration to Istanbul.
***

Migration from Syria to Turkey and Main Areas of Concern

(66) Fikret Elma (Celal Bayar University) and Ahmet Şahin (Celal Bayar University)

Events began in Syria in March 11 within per-spektive of popular uprising called "Arap Spring" has turned into a great chaos and civil war in a very short time. The civil war has brought a wave of mass immigration, a great human tragedy and security issues. İn this context, the close to ten million Syrian is directed internal and external migration. Turkey is one of the neigboring coun-try affected in the first instance from the waves of immigratin in question. As it known sudden and massive migration in Turkey, As well as hu-manitarian respect, undouptly political, social and security aspect has been highly important.
***

Anti-Immigrant Discourse towards Syrians in Turkey: A Neglected Dimension of Syrian Crisis

(83) Nazlı Sıla Cesur (University of Essex) and Deniz Eroğlu (Trakya University)

The growing number of Syrian refugees have been flowing into neighboring countries because of the political conflict happening in Syria. Turkey is one of those in which Syrians have sought refuge since 2011. From the first day of Syrians arrived in this country, Turkey has followed an open –door policy and offered humanitarian assistance for them. In this regard, migration policy of Turkey towards mass influx of Syrians has received a tepid applause from different stakeholders in the field.

Although many Syrians are hosted in 22 refugee camps in Turkey, a great number of them have become to live outside of refugee camps in certain provinces. Today, it is highly possible to see Syrian refugees in the streets of big cities, like Istanbul or Ankara, begging and trying to survive under very poor conditions. Since their stay in Turkey has lasted more than it was expected and the presence of Syrians has become visible, the encounter between local people and Syrians has turned into daily practice. These face to face encounters, between the Syrians and local people, have created another important issue to address " the growing negative attitudes and discrimination towards Syrians". These approach towards Syrians are highly intensified by "the rumors" about them. Some of remarkable examples are 'Syrians were granted citizenship in return for voting for the Justice and Development Party in the elections"; "jobs are offered for the Syrians";

"Syrians spread disease across the region." Eventually, these claims have shaped the perspectives and interactions between Syrians and local people.

Focusing on these 'rumors' and their impacts on perspectives and interactions between Syrians and local people, this paper will analyse a neglected dimension of Syrian crisis: anti-immigrant discourse have dramatically developed towards Syrians. Giving an insight into the society since post- Syrian crisis, the analysis of the anti-immigrant discourses can provide in identifying prospective policy-solutions on unprecedented mass influx crisis.

***

Turkey as a Host Country: Turkish Public Opinion towards Syrian Refugees and Domestic Politics

(127) Juliette Tolay (Penn State Harrisburg)

The study of anti-immigrant feelings has so far been divided between statistical analysis of survey data and historico-institutional approaches to understand the broader factors that explain attitudes towards immigrants. Increasingly attention – and similar approaches – has been applied to newly countries of immigration. This paper argues that in newer countries of immigration, where opinion and attitudes towards immigration have not yet taken a permanent form, insufficient

attention has been paid to the short-term impact of daily politics. The empirical analysis of this paper is based on the ongoing inflows of Syrian refugees in Turkey. Turkey has become an important – and unintentional – country of immigration, yet the Turkish public remains largely unaware of this situation. The estimated 1.5 million Syrian refugees who have come to the country since 2011 have led to a new public discourse on refugees. This paper tracks this new public discourse through an analysis of Turkish social media (Twitter): it looks both at the quantity and nature of social media statements on Syrian refugees, and link this evolution with the Turkish domestic agenda. The analysis highlights the impact that domestic politics has on the perception of refugees, even when domestic issues do not relate directly with refugees issues.
***

SESSION 9B – Edebiyatta Göç ve Kimlik

Edebiyatta Göçmen Kimliğine Sıradışı Bir Bakış: Kati Hirşel

(65) Pınar Güzelyürek Çelik (Yıldız Teknik University) and Lale Özcan (Yıldız Teknik University)

Yükseköğretim yapmak amacıyla gitmiş olduğu Almanya'da uzun yıllar kalan Esmahan

Aykol, Almanya'da bir Türk olarak yaşadığı travmatik deneyimlerin sonucunda, maruz kaldığı ayrımcılığın yaratmış olduğu "intikam ve öfke" duygularını sosyal düzlemde kabul gören yaratıcılık alanına yönelterek yüceltmiş ve böylelikle Türkiye'de yaşayan bir Alman karakteri kurgulayarak kaleme aldığı polisiye romanlarını edebiyat dünyasına kazandırmıştır. Almanya'da Türk bir bilimkadını olarak yaşamış olduğu deneyimleri "Kati Hirşel sayesinde bir Alman da Türkiye'de ayrımcılığa uğruyor diye düşünmeye başladım ve delirmekten kurtuldum" ifadeleriyle açıklayan yazarın bir izdüşümü olarak nitelendirebileceğimiz roman karakteri çok boyutlu, çok katmanlı bir kahraman olarak karşımıza çıkmaktadır.

Sigmund Freud'un psikanalitik kuramında, yüceltme savunma mekanizması, toplumsal olan ile bireysel olan arasındaki huzursuzluk ve gerilimin yarattığı çatışmanın getirdiği bir mekanizma olarak, sanatın, bilimin yani her türlü yaratıcı ve düşünsel etkinliğin kaynağı olarak tanımlanır. Bu mekanizma, kimi kuramcılar tarafından cinsel sapkınlıkların ve komplekslerin bir dışavurumu olarak, bu sorunların yarattığı gerilimin sanat ve düşün yapıtına aktarılması biçiminde tanımlansa da, bireyin yaşadığı travmatik deneyimleri sanata ve düşüne yönlendirilmesi olarak da açıklanmaktadır.

Aykol'un da sık sık dile getirdiği gibi Almanya'da bulunduğu sıralarda maruz kaldığı dışlanmışlık ve ayrımcılık uygulamalarının yöneldiği iki hedef bulunmaktadır: Almanya'da yükseköğretim yapmaya çalışan bir bilimkadını olarak kadın kimliği ve Türk kimliği. Bu iki kimliğe yönelen önyargıları, ayrımcı tutumları Türkiye'de kendi ayakları üstünde durmaya çalışan Alman asıllı bir kitabevi sahibesine yönelterek yazar kanımızca göçmen edebiyatı unsurlarını alışılagelmiş kalıplardan soyutlamış, milletler üstü bir seviyeye çıkararak göçmenlik kavramına farklı bir bakış açısı getirmiştir.

Bu açıdan Esmahan Aykol'u ne birinci ne de ikinci kuşak göçmen edebiyatı yazarlarıyla bir tutabiliriz. Aykol'un polisiye edebiyat seçimi de bizce bu farkı yansıtan özelliklerinden biridir.

Söz konusu çalışmada Esmahan Aykol'un yurtdışında pekçok ödüle layık görülen ve çok satanlar listesinde yer alan polisiye romanları (Kitapçı Dükkanı (2001), Kelepir Ev (2003), Şüpheli bir Ölüm (2007), İstanbul'da Tango (2012)) bu farklı bakış açısını ortaya koymak amacıyla irdelenecektir. Yazarın travmatik deneyimlerini edebiyata yöneltme vurgusu yüceltme mekanizması çerçevesinde ele alınarak, roman kahramanını kendisinin "eş insanı" olarak kurgulamasının izleri takip edilecektir. Ardından Aykol'un roman kurgusu edebiyatta göçmen kimliğinin işlenmesi çerçevesinde irdelenerek edebiyata getirmiş olduğu yeni soluk ortaya konmaya çalışılacaktır. Esmahan Aykol'un gerek göçmenliğe bakış açısı, gerek seçmiş olduğu türün özellikleriyle farklı bir sentez ortaya koyduğu, bu durumu kanıtlayan örneklerle açıklanacaktır.

***

Göçmen Edebiyatında Din ve Kimlik Yansımaları - Fakir Baykurt'un Yarım Ekmek Romanında Din ve Gelenek

(145) İsmail Güllü (Karamanoğlu Mehmetbey University)

1980'li yıllarda göç edebiyatında göçmen edebiyatı (migrants literature) veya yabancıların edebiyatı (foreigners literature) yerine "misafir işçi edebiyatı (guest worker literature/Gastarbeiterliteratur) kavramının daha çok kullanıldığı görülmektedir. İlk zamanlarda Türkçe yazılan Türk göç yazınının son yıllarda ağırlıklı Almanca yazılmaya başlandığı görülmektedir. Almanya'daki Türkiye kökenli yazarlara bakıldığında sadece Türkçe ya da sadece Almanca yazanlar olduğu gibi her iki dilde de edebi eserler veren yazarlara rastlamak mümkündür. Türkiye'deki etnik, dini ve siyasi çeşitlilik Almanya'daki Türklerin eserlerine de yansımış, onların çalışmalarını da çeşitlendirmiştir. Bunun yanında göçmen tecrübesi yaşamanın beraberinde getirdiği bir takım psiko-sosyal özellikler onların çalışmalarında da ortaya çıkar.

Edebiyat eserleri döneminin toplumsal yapısının izlerini taşıyan eserlerdir. Bu anlamda roman, toplumsal gerçekliğin bir yansıması niteliğindedir. Bu yönü ile de sosyoloji bilimi edebi eserleri kullanmalıdır. Roman ile toplumsal yaşam arasındaki güçlü ilişkiyi eserlerine taşıyan Baykurt'un romanları sosyolojik bir çözümleme imkanı sunmaktadır. Yarım Ekmek romanında insanların gündelik hayatlarını etkileyen bir unsur olarak inanç ve ritüeller yoğun bir şekilde yer almaktadır. Yarım Ekmek'te kendisi de bir göçmen olan yazar sadece toplumsal gerçekliği tasvir etmekle yetinmiyor romanı araçsallaştırarak kimi zaman eleştiri ve yönlendirmeler yapıyor ve tipleştirmeler ile açık veya kapalı mesajlar veriyor. Özellikle Türkiye-Almanya karşılaştırmalarında Türkiye'deki o dönem siyasi yapısına ilişkin bir takım eleştiriler açıkça görülür.

Araştırma konusu yaptığımız Fakir Baykurt'un 1997 yılında yayınladığı Yarım Ekmek romanı ile birlikte Koca Ren ve Yüksek Fırınlar'dan oluşan "Duisburg Üçlemesi" adlı üç romanları dış konusunu ele alan romanlarıdır. Yüksek Fırınlar, Duisburg Üçlemesi'nin ilk romanıdır. Bu romanda göç sürecinde birbirinden farklı kültürel ortamlardan beslenmiş birey ve ailelerin çatışması anlatılır. Yazar, muhafazakar bireyler ile muhafazakar olmayan bireyler arasındaki çatışmalar romanın temel konusudur. Duisburg Üçlemesi'nin diğer bir romanı 1986 yılında yayınlanan Koca Ren romanıdır. Yazar, Türk ve Alman eğitim sisteminin farklılığı üzerinden, göç sürecinde Türk çocuklarının bu yeni eğitim sistemine ve kültürel ortama uyum problemlerini merkeze alır. Göç sürecinde öne çıkan en önemli problemlerden biri olan kuşaklar arası farklılaşma ve çatışma konusu romanın en temel teması niteliğindedir. Duisburg Üçlemesinin üçüncü romanı olan Yarım Ekmek romanı 1997 yılında basılmıştır. Diğer iki romandan daha farklı bir üslup ve yaklaşımla dış göç meselesine eğilen Baykurt, bu romanda eşi Türkiye'de ölen ve üç çocukla birlikte yalnız kalan bir kadının (Kezik Acar) Almanya macerası ve daha sonra ölen eşinin kemiklerini Almanya'ya getirip defin etme çabaları sırasında yaşadığı olayları anlatır. Romanda bireysel sorunlar ve kimlik problemleri yanında toplumsal ve kültürel karşılaştırmalara da sıkça yer verilmektedir. Kalıcılık ve geçicilik tartışmaları ekseninde farklı kuşaklar ve farklı dünya görüşüne sahip göçmen Türklerin yaşadığı gelenek, dindarlık ve modern hayata uyum sağlama çabaları içinde kimlik arayışları romanda öne çıkan konuların başında yer alır.

Bu bağlamda sunmayı planladığımız bildiride sosyolojik bir dille göç edebiyatında din ve kimlik unsurunu Fakir Baykurt'un Yarım Ekmek romanı üzerinden analiz etmeyi planlamaktayım.

***

Melezlik ve Bir Eğretileme Olarak Çeviri: Amin Maalouf'un Eserlerinde Kimlik, Aidiyet ve Melezlik Gibi Kavramlar Üzerinde Etnometodolojik Bir İnceleme

(55) Hülya Yılmaz (Yıldız Teknik University) and Füsun Ataseven (Yıldız Teknik University)

Günümüzde melez kimliğini eserlerine yansıtan çok sayıda yazar vardır. Söz konusu yazarlar, çokkültürlü ve çokdilli bir dünyayı hedefleyen toplumumuzun temsilcileri gibidirler. Bununla birlikte bu yazarlar, onları oluşturan geçmişlerini inkâr etmezler. Onların kullandığı dil, çift kimliklerinin gerilim alanıdır adeta, çünkü dil kimliğin en önemli parçasıdır.

Bu çalışma, etnometodolojik yöntemler çerçevesinde ve çeviribilim bakış açısıyla Amin Maalouf'un *Afrikalı Leo* ve *Doğu'dan Uzakta* adlı iki romanında "kimlik" ve "aidiyet" kavramları bağlamında yazarı niteleyen çokkültürlülük ve melezlik olgularının yazıda izlerini sürmeyi hedeflemektedir. Fransızca olarak kaleme aldığı eserlerinde Maalouf, Doğu ve Batı kültürlerini harmanlamış, yazı aracılığıyla kendi melez kimliğini ortaya koymuştur. Etnometodolojinin amacı günlük olgular üzerine yapılan betimlemelerin, raporların, değerlendirmelerin belli bir etkileşim içinde üretilme biçimini incelemek, çözmektir. Böylece yöntemsel bir çalışma gerçekleştirilmiş olur. Çeviribilim bağlamında Berman ve Venutti'nin söylemlerinde 'deneyim olarak yabancı olana bakış', 'öteki'nin kabulü, kavranması' gibi kavramlar, ya da Sömürgecilik-Sonrası söylemde kimlik inşası sürecinde yaşanan dönüşüme çeviri olarak bakılması, "Şarkiyatçılık" (E.Said), "melezlik", "muğlaklık" ve "üçüncü alan" (H. Bhabha) "kimlik" ve "aidiyet" gibi tartışılan kavramlar, Maalouf eserlerinde yapacağımız etnometodolojik çalışmada ele alacağımız temel kavramlar olacaktır. Sömürgecilik ve Sömürgecilik-Sonrası süreçlerinin kişiler üzerindeki psikolojik etkileri, çalışmamızda, kimliğin inşası sürecini etkilemesi bağlamında önemlidir ve bu konuda etnopsikoloji alanında yapılan araştırmalar (Fanon) dikkate alınacaktır. Özetle çalışmamızda sorunsalımız, melez kimlikli bir yazar olan Amin Maalouf'un, aidiyetlerinin toplamından kaynaklanan çokkültürlülük ve çokdillilik özelliklerini eserlerinde görebiliyor muyuz? Zaman içinde dönüştürülmüş/evrilmiş/çevrilmiş olan kimliğinin izlerini eserlerinde nasıl açığa çıkarabiliriz? Sömürgecilik-Sonrası incelemelerin ortaya koyduğu psikolojik etkiler yazıya nasıl yansımıştır? Melezliği bir zenginlik olarak gören Maalouf'un dille olan ilişkisini nasıl değerlendirebiliriz? Sorunsalımız, bu sorular ışığında, melez kişilerde, kimlikler arasındaki gel-gitlerin, dönüşümlerin, çeviribilim ile etnometoloji bilim dalları arasında bağ kurarak, mecazi anlamıyla bir çeviri deneyimi, bir eğretileme olarak görülmesini ve o bağlamda ele alınmasını sağlamaktır.

***

Tuna Dergisi ve Göç Edebiyatına Bir Bakış - Yazar ve Şair Zahit Güney'in Göç ile İlgili Yazıları Üzerine-

(109) Cahit Kahraman (Namık Kemal University) and İlhan Güneş (Republic of Turkey Ministry of National Education)

Bulgaristan Türkleri tarih süreci içerisinde sürekli göç olayları ile karşı karşıya kalmış, yaşadıkları sıkıntılar ve duyguları çeşitli yazılı kaynaklarda dile getirmişlerdir. Araştırmamızı kapsayan Tuna dergisi, göç ve göçmenlerle ilgili yazılara yer vermek amacıyla kurulmuş çok değerli bir kaynak oluşturmaktadır. Tuna dergisi, Mehmet Çavuş tarafından 1996 yılında İstanbul'da kurulmuştur. Yayın hayatına başladıktan sonra sadece göçmenler arasında değil, Türk edebiyatında da önemli yer edinmiştir. Tuna dergisi 3 ayda bir yayınlanan sanat, kültür ve eğitim dergisidir. Kuruluş amacı göç ve göçmenlerin duygu ve düşüncelerini anlatmak ve aktarmak olmuştur. Yazarları çeşitli dönemlerde Bulgaristan'dan göç etmiş, göç anılarını şiirlere ve romanlara dönüştürmüş göçmenlerden oluşmaktadır. Bu eserlerde göç olaylarının sorunları ve bıraktığı izleri görmek mümkün olurken, göçmenlerin iç dünyasını da edebi bir dille aktarmaktadır. Çok doğaldır ki bu göçler Bulgaristan Türklerinin vicdanlarında derin izler bırakmış, bu duygulanmalar çok sayıda Bulgaristanlı Türk yazarı ve şairi bu konuda türlü edebi ürünler kaleme almıştır. Araştırmamızda, Tuna dergisi kuruluş ve amacı hakkında bilgi vermek, ayrıca 1989 yılında Bulgaristan'dan Türkiye'ye göç eden ve halen Tekirdağ'da ikamet eden şair ve yazar Zahit Güney'in yaşamı, edebi kişiliği ve eserlerini incelemek olacaktır. Zahit Güney, Bulgaristan'dan göç etmiş bir yazar ve şair olarak, eserlerinde göç temasını usta bir dille işlemiş, göç edebiyatına hayatını adamış bir yazardır. Eserleri duygu yüklü, içten söylenmiş ve gerçekçidir. Göç sırasında yaşanan sıkıntılar, vatan sevgisi, ulus sevgisi, geçmişe duyulan özlem ve hasret gibi konular ustalıkla ele alınmıştır.

***

SESSION 9C – Education and Migration

Return Migration of Highly Skilled Turkish Origin from Austria to Turkey

(32TP) Hakan Kılıç (Gaziantep University/University of Vienna)

Migration and usually the recent demands for the integration are for a long time on the epicenter of the agenda of national politics and global society. Hence politicians are discussing about paths and way outs of the problem of integration. Still, it's an open issue whether and to what extent the acquisition of a new language and culture in diaspora will lead to anticipated results.

Starting therefore, the immigration from less developed regions to Europe is increasingly perceived as a problem. Nevertheless, and despite the economic times of crises, Europe is still gaining attractiveness and is perceived as 'welfare zone'. Therefore, the discussions about qualified immigration are top theme, because the absorption capacity is an obvious trouble.

A 'phenomenon' that increasingly occurs in this regard in the last few years in Central European countries, however, is neglected especially in Austria is the return migration/intention of university graduates of Turkish origin. In spite of the fact that highly qualified immigrants are more able to integrate their selves into the society, it can be assumed that the return intention of highly qualified Turkish origin persons will increase and the less qualified will tend to stay. In migration research this process is called as a 'squandering of human capital' or 'brain drain' from developed countries. Further, these new category of migrants – who shows hybrid identities - are able to act as 'bridge people', who can afford to successful integration work in Austria. In the final decision to return migration, influential factors as the question of identity, labor market integration or belonging are playing essential roles.

I will theorize as above and discuss this new category of international migration, with a view to Turkish (Austro-Turkish) community in Austria.

***

Educational Achievement of Turkish Immigrants' Children in Europe: A Comparative Study of United Kingdom and Belgium

(5) Serkan Baykuşoğlu (University of Eastern Finland) and Orhan Ağırdağ (University of Amsterdam)

Turkish speaking students perform significantly low at both the primary and secondary levels in UK and Belgium. Their academic achievements fall behind their native peers including other migrant groups. The purpose of this study is to provide insights about the educational achievements of Turkish Speaking children in compulsory education in United Kingdom and Belgium in a comparative perspective.

Belgium has one of the highest performance differences in Europe between children, and second generation immigrant children achieve lower than the first generation immigrant children. Although educational differences between native, European and Asian students disappeared, the gap remained for Moroccan and Turkish immigrant children in Belgium.

In UK, Turkish speaking pupils' achievements are disturbingly low when compared with their native counterparts and other migrant groups such as Bangladeshi and Somali pupils. This is due to a number of factors including language difficulties, socio-economic and parental factors.

The focus of this paper is to draw a general picture of the situation: to determine factors affecting Turkish speaking educational achievement; to identify challenges and strategies; and to recommend solutions for improvements in both countries. This study is based on the relevant literature review, educational achievement statistics and government reports.
***

How Education System and Schooling Affect Immigrant Turkish Families' Children on Their Achievement: Comparison of Germany and United Kingdom

(6) Aslıgül Aysel (Ruhr-University Bochum) and Serkan Baykuşoğlu (University of Eastern Finland)

Education has been considered a way of social advancement for working families. This comparative study focuses on Turkish immigrant families in Europe. Most of them have low skills and a low educational level and thus education means a unique opportunity for social mobility for their children. Achievement in the education system would allow their children to obtain higher career and higher status within the society. This achievement gaps are shown to be particularly relevant when considering the status of new generation immigrants who were born, socialised and educated in the host country and who are thus supposed to share the same opportunities as natives. Turkish immigrants' children underachieve in compulsory education as large differentials have been observed between Turkish speaking children and those who do not come from this background. Their academic attainment falls behind their native peers, and it is lowest among other immigrant groups.

The aim of this study is to provide insights about the educational achievements of Turkish immigrants' children in mainstream education in Germany and United Kingdom in a comparative perspective. One of the factors affecting the educational achievement of Turkish migrants is the effectiveness of host country's educational system and institutions. It is aimed to find out how educational systems' mechanisms affect immigrant children performance. Another essential aspect is the wish for the socio-ecenomic advancement of the concerned. The study provides a survey of the literature on the determinants of the educational achievement of Turkish immigrant children at an individual, scholastic and country level. Furthermore it presents research objectives, data and methodology.

It was followed by presenting the results of analysis. Finally, this study reports conclusion and suggests possible future directions for Turkish immigrants' children.
***

Kurdish American Students and Parents in Nashville Public Schools: Challenges, Needs, Experiences, and Expectations

(9) Demet Arpacık (The City University of New York)

Kurdish people are the third largest ethnic group in Nashville Public Schools. This qualitative study investigated the experiences of 15 students from middle school, high school, and college as they lived and attended school in the United States. The study also reached to 17 parents to more holistically understand the experiences of an immigrant family (15 of whom are parents of student interviewees). Two semi-structured qualitative interview protocols were used to explore the needs and expectations of Kurdish American students and their parents related to the education system. This study also aimed at understanding the challenges that they faced related to school. As students and parents talked about their experiences, the following themes emerged for students and parents: For students (1) religion as a barrier and identity, (2) strong attachment to and respect for Kurdish culture and family values, (3) cultural segregation, and (4) cultural representation at school. The themes that emerged from parents' interviews, which were complementary with the themes from student interviews, were; (1) satisfaction with the system, (2) lack of understanding the system, (3) fears related to their children.

***

SESSION 9D – Conflict and Politics in Kurdish Migration

Contributor or Barrier: Role of the Kurdish Diaspora in Turkey's European Union Accession Process

(104) Sevin Gülfer Sağnıç (Boğaziçi University)

International migration has led to the creation of new actors and channels for politics which have increased the interconnectedness of states. One such actor, the Kurdish diaspora in Europe, is a well-organized and highly political diaspora that has tried to use its inter-connectedness to achieve political objectives in Turkey. Turkey's European Union accession process created a vital opportunity to rouse criticisms such as the possibility of using human rights criteria as a point against Turkey's accession. This study aims to analyse the role of the Kurdish diaspora and its activities in Turkey's European Union accession process through focusing on the importation of the Kurdish question into Europe through Kurdish migration. It is argued that, the diaspora is both a barrier and a contributor for the accession process; it wants Turkey to

join the EU and spends effort on the continuation of the process but it does not want to Turkey to join without solving the Kurdish question in a democratic way and so barriers the process in terms of enforcing the EU to not to accept the Turkey's membership without a peaceful solution to the Kurdish question. The efforts of the diaspora are not fruitless; they are affecting the bilateral relations of the EU members and Turkey as well as the accession process. Through analysing the progress reports on Turkey (1998, 1999, 2000, 2011, 2012, 2013) in parallel to consolidation and activities of the diaspora this paper discusses the formation of the Kurdish diaspora in Europe and its means and activities vis-à-vis the changes in Europe's approach towards the question of Turkish-Kurdish relations. Additionally, interviews had been used to map the current position and activities of the leading diaspora institutions in Brussels. This study is a part of growing body of research on transnationalism and diaspora studies.
***

Media Use and Understandings of Conflict: Turkish and Kurdish Adolescents and Young Adults in London and Istanbul

(35) Kevin Smets (University of Antwerp)

There has been an increased interest in the relations between media and conflict, in media and communication studies as well as in the fields of international relations and peace and development studies. While hitherto the emphasis has mainly been on news reporting, coverage of particular conflicts and the role of media in shaping opinions, much is still to be discovered about how media (mass media as well as online and participatory media) are employed to make meaning of conflict situations and to cope with post-conflict conditions. In the particular case of the Kurdish conflict in Turkey, Başer and Çelik (2014) for instance demonstrate how media play a significant role when it comes to young people and their framings of conflict and imaginations of peace. Inspired by these new avenues in the study of the social and cultural aspects of conflicts, this paper focuses on media use and understandings of conflicts among Turkish and Kurdish adolescents and young adults in two cosmopolitan settings, London and Istanbul. The qualitative data include participant observations in different community centres and cultural organizations, 10 focus group conversations on media use and conflict with adolescents and young adults with Kurdish roots in both cities as well as expert interviews with media producers (journalists, editors). The discussion of these data mainly revolves around 3 issues: (1) the experience of dominant media frames and ways to formulate alternate frames; (2) the role of media use in the making and overcoming of boundaries between different ethnic, political-ideological and religious groups; and (3) the potential of fiction (TV dramas, cinema, short films) to foster understanding of conflict.

***

Under the Surface. A History of Czech Interest in the Kurds

(122) Petr Kubálek

Although Kurdish Studies have officially never existed in Czechoslovakia and the two countries that replaced it in 1993, viz. Czech Republic and Slovakia, the local contributions to the research of the Kurds are important to this day: geographer Josef Wünsch (1842–1907) was the first to locate the sources of the Euphrates and the Tigris and collected ethnographic material from Kurds and Armenians; Iranian Kurdish politician and academic Abdul Rahman Ghassemlou (1930–1989) spent two decades of his life in Prague and wrote a valuable description of traditional rural economy in Kurdistan; and, filmmaker Petr Zrno (born 1946) shot probably the largest documentary film so far on Yezidism. Apart from research and documentation, there have been Czech demonstrations of solidarity with the Kurdish cause, such as a petition signed in 1990 by the then Czechoslovak President Václav Havel (1936–2011).

***

Gendered Experiences of War, Displacement, and Statelessness. A Kurdish Family on the Run.

(132) Wendelmoet Hamelink, Leiden University

In this paper, I focus on the experiences and memories of war and displacement of a Kurdish family currently living in Germany. I investigate their gendered experiences and the cross-border lives they live between Germany, Turkey and Iraqi Kurdistan. Each of the family members has a different story to tell about how they dealt with war and displacement and the shocking events they lived through. Their story did not end with their stay in Germany, but continued through repeated experiences of conflict while traveling to their home region. Also while in Germany, they strongly relate to what happens in their home region, and continue to be involved in its ongoing unstability. The family originates from a village in the far South East of Turkey, located exactly on the Turkey/Iraq border. Bahar, her husband Cengiz, and their eldest daughter Narîn, are singers who are well educated in the oral tradition of their village. In my dissertation I discussed the embodied relationship between musical memories and the individual and collective past, and I argued that their knowledge obtained a different meaning in the diaspora. This paper is based on additional research with the same family. Using life history interviews and long-term research contact as the data for this paper, I show the differences between a male and female perspective on the same events. What consequences did statelessness and displacement have for each of them? How did and do they relate to their memories and cope with trauma and loss? Do they experience Germany as a safe place to live, and how do they relate to the raging war in their home region? The long-term perspective of the paper hopes to shed light on ongoing and repeated experiences of conflict. From the perspective of the stateless, war and illegality become normalized. This has deep consequences for women's lives and subjectivities.

***

Author Index

232

www.gocdergisi.com
www.migrationletters.com
www.tplondon.com
www.turkishmigration.com